**THE BOOK
OF AMUWAPI**

THE BOOK OF

CHRISTOPHER LORD

AMUWAPI

ILLUSTRATED BY PETR NIKL

TWISTED SPOON PRESS / PRAGUE / 2000

Copyright © Christopher Lord, 2000
Illustrations copyright © Petr Nikl, 2000
© Twisted Spoon Press, 2000

All rights reserved. No part of this book may be used or reproduced in any form, save for purposes of review, without the permission of the publisher.

ISBN 80-86264-14-9

**AMUWAPI WEEPS FOR YOU
AND HERE IS THE SHADOW OF HIS SHADOW**

*Inscription on the edge of a sundial
whose markings have been obliterated by blown sand.*

Taklamikan Desert, 4th Millennium BC

AMUWAPI AND THE CATFISH

There was once a catfish, who lived in the deep dark waters of a deep dark pool hidden in the depths of a deep dark forest. The catfish was very old, and very wise, but he was lonely, for he lived alone, and had few opportunities for conversation. One night, the full moon shone on the calm surface of the deep dark pool; and the catfish, lying awake, looked up at the great white circle in the sky.

"Amuwapi," he called out suddenly; "Amuwapi! If it is true that you are still living in the palace of the moon, then I beg you to come and talk with me, for now I am very lonely."

A light wind made the leaves on the trees in the forest rustle, and made the surface of the water of the deep dark pool stir and ripple, so that the reflection of the moon broke into a million glimmering fragments.

"Catfish," said a voice that was the wind and was not the wind, "I am Amuwapi, and I have come to talk with you."

"They say," said the catfish, "that you can grant the things we most desire. So tell me, is it true?"

The wind sighed in the trees.

"I am Amuwapi," said Amuwapi, "and I may grant all things."

"In that case," said the catfish, "I will ask for what I desire most. That is my request to you, Amuwapi."

"A request," said Amuwapi, after he had thought about what the catfish had said, "is not quite the same thing as a wish or a desire; but still, I will do my best. Now, what is it that you most desire?"

"I wish I knew," said the catfish. "For many long years, I have lain in the slime and darkness of this isolated pond, wondering to myself precisely that. Please tell me, Amuwapi: what is it that I most desire?" And the catfish flicked its tail in the mud of its pond.

"I will think about your question," said Amuwapi to the catfish. "But first, I must tell you that I will require something from you in return."

"What is that?" said the catfish.

"I am very bored sitting in the palace of the moon," said Amuwapi; "And I would like to hear a story to amuse me."

"Well that is very easy," said the catfish. "For there is only one story I know."

"Is it an interesting story?" said Amuwapi.

"Well, you can hardly expect me to know that," said the catfish, "since there is no other story with which I could compare it."

"Then we will have to judge it on its own merits," said Amuwapi. "Proceed."

"Very well," said the catfish. "The name of this story is *Amuwapi at the Beginning of the World*."

AMUWAPI AT THE BEGINNING OF THE WORLD*

At the beginning of the world, Amuwapi was alone.

After many, many years had passed, a frog saw Amuwapi weeping.
"Why are you weeping, Amuwapi?" said the frog.
"I am weeping because I don't know what to do," said Amuwapi.
"That's easy," said the frog. "You can be like me. I will teach you to swim in the river."
But Amuwapi did not want to swim in the river like a frog, so he called his brother, and he said "Oh my brother, go with this frog and learn." And so Amuwapi's brother learned to swim like a frog, and he was happy. But Amuwapi was still alone.

After many more years had passed, a deer saw Amuwapi weeping.
"Why are you weeping, Amuwapi?" said the deer.
"I am weeping because I don't know what to do."
"Then come with me and I will teach you to run like the wind."
But Amuwapi did not want to run like the wind, so he called his sister, and he said, "Oh my sister, go with this deer and learn." So Amuwapi's sister learned to run like the wind, and she was happy. But Amuwapi was still alone.

After many more years had passed, an ant saw Amuwapi weeping.
"Why are you weeping, Amuwapi?" said the ant.
"Because I don't know what to do."
"That's easy. Come with me and I will teach you to walk an invisible path."
"That would be useful," said Amuwapi, "but I do not want to learn to walk an invisible path. I will call my father."

---

*Adapted from J. J. Dunleavy, *The Hill Peoples of the Interior*, Kuala Lumpur, 1874 (private press; facsimile no. RH35, Dunleavy Bequest, Trinity College Library, Dublin; Chapter 4: "Their Myths And Legends"). With thanks to Father Crispin J. O'Toole, S. J..

And so Amuwapi called his father. And after many, many more years had passed, all the animals in the forest had come to see why Amuwapi was weeping, and all the fish in the river had come to see why Amuwapi was weeping, and all the insects and spiders and centipedes had come to see why Amuwapi was weeping; and Amuwapi's brothers and sisters, and their brothers and sisters, and all their children and their children's children and their children's children's children had learned all that the animals and the fish and the insects and spiders and centipedes could teach them; and Amuwapi had become a great king, in a palace made of mountains and the ocean. But still he could not stop weeping.

After many, many years, the sun saw Amuwapi weeping.

"I have watched you weeping ever since the beginning of the world," said the sun.

"I do not know what to do," said Amuwapi.

"I know," said the sun. "I cannot help you. But I will help your brothers and your sisters, and their children and their children's children and their children's children's children. They see you weeping, Amuwapi, and they have learned to weep themselves. I will hide my face in shame at your weeping, Amuwapi, so that they may have a rest from looking at you."

And the night came.

In the morning, the sun saw that Amuwapi was still weeping.

"Are you not ashamed, oh Amuwapi, to weep like this?" said the sun.

"I am ashamed," said Amuwapi. "But now I will tell you something. A very, very long time ago, there was a frog who asked me to swim, and there was a deer who asked me to run, and there was an ant who asked me to follow an invisible path; but I did not want to do any of these things. But now you have shown me to hide my face, so that my brothers and my sisters, and their brothers and sisters, and their children, and their children's children, and their children's children's children, will not learn to weep from me; and now I will learn from you."

So Amuwapi left the forest and the river behind. He left his palace made of mountains and the ocean, and he made a home for himself in the palace of the moon. He came out sometimes to see how his brothers and sisters were living without him, but he always waited until the sun had gone down, so they would not see his face: for he was still weeping.

And his tears became the stars, and his weeping became the thunder and the whirlwind. Many, many years have passed. But Amuwapi is still alone.

Roman votive shield with six tears of Amuwapi forming the apices of an invisible six-pointed star.

At the end of the catfish's story, there was a deep dark silence, and everything was very still. After he had thought about what the catfish had said, Amuwapi laughed sadly.

"Tell me," he said gently. "Why are there no catfish in your story?"

"I don't know," said the catfish. "Do some stories have catfish in them, then?"

"Oh, there are some such stories, I dare say," said Amuwapi, "but I cannot remember any of them at present. And anyway, now there is the question of our exchange. I know what is in your mind, catfish, for there is nothing you can keep secret from me. When I have told you what it is you most desire, you plan to ask me to produce it for you. It is not a bad plan, but I must tell you now that what you most desire is something I cannot give you; I cannot make it for you; and I cannot bring it into being for you."

"Then I will never have it," said the catfish.

"It is love," said Amuwapi, "that you most desire. But you must find it by yourself. That is all I have to tell you."

There was a long silence, while the catfish thought about what Amuwapi had said.

"I have lived in this deep dark pool, hidden in the depths of the deep dark forest, for many years now," said the catfish, "and I have never yet found love lying hereabouts."

"You must search," said Amuwapi, "very patiently. But now you must forgive me, for I must return to my weeping."

"Very well," said the catfish; "and I will begin to search for love, since that, after all, is what I most desire."

And that was the end of the catfish's conversation with Amuwapi. Many, many years have passed; but ever since that day, the catfish has never stopped searching for love: and who knows? Perhaps one day he will find it.

AMUWAPI Prehistoric deity: the Weeping God. It seems that the cult of Amuwapi was active in pre-literate and proto-literate SUMER, though some authorities would place its origins in a much more widespread NEOLITHIC or even PALAEOLITHIC religion or cult, traces of which are said to survive in folk cultures and religious iconography across a huge geographical area (spread through migrations and the diffusion of cultures). Mesopotamian records provide some evidence of a pre-Akkadian CREATION MYTH, in which Amuwapi, the Weeping God, plays a central role. However, these records are at best ambiguous, and links with later (or earlier) mythologies are difficult to prove. Amuwapi and his cognates are associated with tears and lamentation, with human sacrifice (and especially with the removal of the head, heart and hands of the victim during such sacrifice), and, in the Near Eastern records at least, also with writing and with the sundial. In some texts, there is evidence that there was a body of astronomy and astrology associated with the cult, and it has been speculated that this was transmitted to early Dynastic EGYPT. It is therefore supposed to provide a missing link between Egyptian, Sumero-Akkadian and MESOAMERICAN religions. Support for this hypothesis has come from the decipherment of the HARRAPA glyphs of the Indus Valley, and from the recovery of some apparently related artefacts from lost cities in South Arabia and Central Asia. In its most developed form, the "Amuwapi hypothesis" (famously promoted in Klipsten and Dunleavy's classic *The Amuwapi Cycle*, Blackwell's, Oxford, 1963) suggests that the Indus Valley texts are indicative of a cultural spread to ancient CHINA and the Far East. Interpretations of isolated texts and artefacts, such as evidence of a (mechanical) statue of a weeping god in Alexandria, or of Klipsten and Dunleavy's mass of anecdotal and folkloric evidence from around the world, have unfortunately now done as much to obscure the true nature of the supposed Amuwapi religion as to illuminate it. One ingenious hypothesis which is worth mentioning is that it was writing that caused the cult's extinction, despite the fact that the cult itself was the original reason for the development and spread of writing in the first place.

— C. J. O'T.

Encyclopedia of World Religion
(Chicago and Amsterdam, 1957–83)
Vol. I, Aa'a to Aspirationalism

THE THREE SACRED THINGS

The Commentary says: What are the sacred things? Why are they sacred? This is our answer.

THE FIRST SACRED THING IS THE SUNDIAL.

We know that Amuwapi hides his face from the light of the sun, and so all shadows remind us of Amuwapi; as the darkness and the night reminds us of Amuwapi. But shadows are a commonplace thing.

We know that Amuwapi was alone at the beginning of the world; and so the passage of time reminds us of Amuwapi; as the changes of the seasons remind us of Amuwapi; as the alternation of day and night and the cycle of the sun's movement in the sky in the course of the year reminds us of Amuwapi. But the passage of time is a commonplace thing.

The Commentary says: Although there is both light and darkness, and although there is a world of light and a world of darkness, and although the world of light and the world of darkness have been separated since before the beginning of the world, we see in shadows that even in light there is darkness; and even in darkness there is light. Although there is both permanence and change; although there is a world that changes and a world that does not change; and although the world that changes and the world that does not change have been separated since before the beginning of the world; still we see in the movement of shadows that even in change there is permanence, and even in permanence there is change. That is how we should interpret this part of the description of the first sacred thing.

The sundial shows us the difference between light and darkness; it shows us the difference between permanence and change. It shows us that everything will one day return to what it was before. It shows us that what grows will be diminished; and that what is diminished will grow. It shows us the year with its parts and its divisions, which are nothing but change: but the sundial itself neither grows, nor diminishes, nor changes. The sundial itself is neither light nor dark. The sundial is not a commonplace thing. That is why the sundial is sacred.

The Commentary says: *And it is by the sundial that we learn the correct and true times and days for the sacrifices. Otherwise we would not know.*

THE SECOND SACRED THING IS THE MENSTRUATION OF WOMEN.

We know that at the beginning of the world, Amuwapi was alone; but now the world is full of a thousand things; and so generation reminds us of Amuwapi; as the union of male and female reminds us of Amuwapi. But generation is a commonplace thing.

We know that Amuwapi lives alone in the Palace of the Moon; and so the womb, where the foetus lives alone and hides his face from the world, reminds us of Amuwapi. But the womb is a commonplace thing.

We know that the tears of Amuwapi feed the day and the night; and all the thousand things that live in the world are fed like this; and so the red blood reminds us of Amuwapi; as everything that flows and drips like tears reminds us of Amuwapi. But blood is a commonplace thing.

The Commentary says: *It is asked, Why do some of the thousand things depend on the union of male and female, and others not? Why do some of the thousand things depend on blood, and others not? To which we reply: There are some things, such as frogs and flies and certain birds, which do not rely on the union of male and female for their generation; and there are some things, such as trees and clouds, which, though alive, do not require the flow of blood. But these things do not suffer as we do. That is the difference.*

The menstruation of women is a weeping of tears of blood from the darkness and loneliness of the womb out into the world of light and the world of the thousand things. It shows us the difference between youth and age; it shows us the difference between suffering and joy. Amuwapi must hide his tears from his children and his children's children and his children's children's children; and the woman is ashamed of her menstruation too, and hides in pain and loneliness and darkness. The menstruation of women is not a commonplace thing. That is why the menstruation of women is sacred.

The Commentary says: *And when there is no sundial, and in the winter when the sun does not shine, it is by the menstruation of women that we know time is still passing. Otherwise, we would not know.*

THE THIRD SACRED THING IS WRITING.

We know that Amuwapi spoke with the birds and the animals and all the thousand things, and so words remind us of Amuwapi; as the voices of children, that do not use words, remind us of Amuwapi — for before the words there are thoughts and feelings: and the cry of the new-born reminds us that Amuwapi suffers as we do. But words and cries are commonplace things.

We know that shadows remind us of Amuwapi; and the marks of writing are the shadows of words; as words are the shadows of thoughts and feelings; as thoughts and feelings are the shadows of suffering. But shadows are a commonplace thing.

We know that at the beginning of the world Amuwapi was alone; and so the world was empty; and when the thousand things came to talk with Amuwapi, then the world was no longer empty; and when we write we take what is empty, and after we have written, it is no longer empty. But emptiness is a commonplace thing.

The Commentary says: *It is asked, What is written? We answer: the story of Amuwapi at the beginning of the world is written. That is why we say that writing is the shadow of Amuwapi.*

Writing teaches us the difference between what is and what is not. It is the shadow of a shadow of a shadow: but shadows change and writing — which is nothing but the shadow of a shadow — does not change. In the sacrifice of animals, we study their markings, both inside and outside; and it is said that our writing has the same meaning as the markings of the thousand things. Writing is not a commonplace thing. That is why writing is sacred.

The Commentary says: *It is asked, Why is it sometimes impossible to interpret the markings of the thousand things? Is the suffering of the world hidden from our understanding? We answer: We can understand our own writing, since it is the shadow of the shadow of our own thoughts and feelings. But the markings of the thousand things, whether they are dead, or alive, or dying, are not the shadow of the shadow of our own thoughts and feelings, but instead they are the shadow of the shadow of the suffering of the world. We know that only Amuwapi is in a position to comprehend all the suffering of the world, and that is because at the beginning of the world he was alone, as we are not. So if we sometimes do not understand the markings of animals or of other things, then it is because we still do not have sufficient experience and knowledge of the world. It is not because the markings themselves are without meaning. It is the same thing when we show our own writing to a child, who makes sounds but does not understand the use of words. If he could speak, then he would say: This writing is without meaning.*

*I am the shadow of a shadow of a shadow,
and my blood is nothing but a teardrop*

FORMULA TO BE REPEATED BY THE VICTIM AT A SACRIFICE.

Duplex Ægyptiorum principium bonum et malum.
After an engraving in *Antiqvitates Graecae et Romanæ*,
P. Montfaucon, Nürnberg, MDCCLVII.

FRAGMENT FROM A LOST CITY

... and Amuwapi spoke in a dream to Ursalim in his sadness, saying "What is there in a poet's life that can compare with my sadness?" And Ursalim answered: "Today, in the market place, I saw the daughter of the merchant Bassari; and she turned her great black eyes on me, and my heart was poisoned with love. And now, in my madness, I do not love my friends. I do not love the nightingale that sings in the courtyard. I do not love my wine or my cakes of honey. I love only the coal black eyes of the merchant Bassari's beautiful daughter. And yet I know that she will never be mine, for I am nothing but a poet and a madman, and she is the daughter of the wealthy merchant Bassari. And in my madness, I do not sleep a natural sleep. Instead, my sleep is filled with dreams of strange gods and demons; and among them is the great god Amuwapi, who asks me: What is there in a poet's life that can compare to my sadness? And I have no answer to give him." And Amuwapi said to Ursalim in his dream: "You are a fortunate man. For tomorrow the beautiful daughter of the merchant Bassari will smile on you again; and your tears will be as fresh as the morning dew." And the poet Ursalim lamented until dawn.

Forschungen zur südarabischen Epigraphie, Band 44, Lieferung CXVI, Berlin, 1926.

A THEOLOGICAL DISCUSSION

A priest of Amuwapi introduces some basic concepts to a new arrival at the temple.

Now this is the main sundial, you see, which is really terribly important. The whole organization of everything ultimately depends on this, so make sure you study it all very carefully. If you look here, you'll see that the shadow here moves like this over here round to this line here over the first part of the year, up to the midsummer sacrifices, I mean, and then back along here for the second part of the year. So the main sacrifices are all marked out along here, with these marks for how many victims there should be, you see? Five here, three over here . . . This is the new year . . . Well, they'll tell you all about it, so don't worry if it all looks a bit complicated at first. Actually, we do have another system for the moon as well, but it's not so difficult to keep up with it, because I mean you just have to look at it, don't you, to see if it's full or half-full or whatever it is, and anyway all it does really is mark the times for killing the first-born, you know. All right? So anyway, that's the practical basis of it all, apart from the eclipses and the tides and all that, but as I say they'll tell you all about that later. Now, over here we have the House of Menstruation. I suppose you know more or less how that's organized. We have a Mother of Menstruation who runs the place, and basically all the paid-up members send us their wives and daughters once a month for confinement. We have separate quarters for servants, around there, but you can't actually see them from here; and funnily enough we have a rule which says they're allowed to bring a servant as long as the servant isn't menstruating herself. Makes it all too complicated, apparently, although I don't really understand why. Apparently there's a danger that they might fight among themselves. Anyway, you can't go in of course but you can see it's built around a central courtyard, which is where they do all the menstruation rituals, screaming, tearing animals apart, smearing each other with blood, you know, all that sort of thing. If there's anything you need to know, you can ask the Mother of Menstruation. OK? Now . . . here we have the main sacrificial table. Well, I'm sure you've seen it all a hundred times. We stand here, knife goes in here, head comes off here, hands over there . . . This is for the entrails, the heart goes into this basket here . . . Well, you know about that. Any questions? Good. I don't suppose you've . . . No. Of course not. Not just yet. Yes, it is quite exciting, I suppose, the first time, especially, but you get used to it, you know. And a lot does depend on the victim, as you can imagine. Some are more cooperative than others, you know. And do make sure that everything is nice and sharp! Sharp sharp sharp! Otherwise it can create a very bad impression, you see. Upsets the relations, too. Anyway, Don't Worry, that's the main thing. You can always warm up on the first-born, and it's just a sort of knack. And frankly, between you and me, it's not the end of the world if we do have a few nasty moments now and again. Atmosphere, you know! I mean, we are supposed to represent a religion of eternal suffering, aren't we? Yes . . . What? Oh yes, of course, I was coming to that. Our basic beliefs, all that. Yes. Let's just sit down over here for a bit, shall we, and I'll . . . there. That's for disembowelling, by the way, over there. Not much call for it nowadays, though. Pity really. Where was I? Oh yes. Now, I expect you know the basics, so I . . . Oh. Oh, I see. Quite. Well, look, in that case, let's start at the beginning, shall we? Now, our basic position – and I'll go out on a limb here and say that this is really where we do differ from a lot of other people – is that we basically believe that suffering is a good thing, and therefore that the more of it there is in the world the better. Yes. Yes. That's right. Yes. But the thing is, isn't it, that this principle doesn't actually apply directly to us. The priests. Good Lord no. And the justification for that, of course, is that being very dedicated and devoted ourselves, you see, then if we actually tried to suffer as much as possible ourselves, we basically wouldn't be in any position to help anyone else with their suffering, now would we? Help *them* to suffer, I mean. We wouldn't have time for it, would we, apart from anything else. So, oh dear, we have to deny ourselves personal suffering in order to serve the higher purpose of helping everyone else to suffer as much as possible. And that's your basic duty as a priest, you see. Actually, technically, what it is is a special kind of sacrifice that you're expected to make, as a priest, that is, which is why we have that symbolic child sacrifice when you're accepted into the priesthood. It symbolizes the death of your own suffering. All the suffering that you are actually sacrificing yourself by joining the priesthood. And of course it's a lifelong duty. We choose a child because as you know children are the most sinful and guilty, since they have not had so long to purify themselves by suffering. So, we do encourage everyone to make children suffer particularly. But anyway, I'm sure that's all perfectly clear, isn't it? Good. So let's talk a little now about this central idea we have of suffering, just to make sure you've got that clear in your mind too. Now, as you know, we believe that the entire universe consists of suffering and nothing else. We particularly admire menstruation because it reminds us of the essential link between suffering and the continuity of the universe, which we interpret by saying that pain and time are identical, you see. From a philosophical perspective, I mean. The real suffering in the world is all just the image of this basic all-encompassing suffering, which, again from a theoretical point of view, you understand, we describe as the suffering of Amuwapi. But of course then we make a basic distinction between what we call the *pain* of Amuwapi and the *tears* of Amuwapi. The pain is more the sort of spiritual aspect of it, and the tears mean the physical world, you know, birds, animals, people, all that sort of thing. So when we examine the sundial, for instance, then that tells us about the tears primarily, you see – the physical manifestation of Amuwapi's suffering. It shows us the physical revolutions of everything in the universe, everything in the sky; but it's just what you could call the mechanical aspect of things, you see. And what we try and do is to put the spiritual aspect of things back in, to keep everything balanced, and the basic technique we have is to produce what you could call concentrations of suffering at key points of the year, matching the divisions of the physical year, as revealed to us by the sundial. You see? I hope this is clear enough. Good. Oh, yes, ask away. Please. The main thing is for you to get it all straight in your mind. No? No questions? Well, where was I, then . . . Ah yes. Now, while we are in general terms very keen on suffering in all its forms, we have been forced to compromise when it comes to death itself. What we say about *that* is that it's a grace only permitted to the sacrificial victims, you see. Now I realize that on the face of it that might seem a bit peculiar, but there's a simple practical reason for it. It's actually a reaction to too much belief, strange as that may seem. Too much truth, you could say, although we do actually keep a bit quiet about that aspect of it. You see, in the past we've sometimes had to deal with whole large groups of believers just suddenly vanishing in a surprise outbreak of religious sentiment. Yes: touching, isn't it? Moving. They go to extraordinary lengths to make sure that it's all as painful as possible, too, as a rule. Well, all that sort of thing is admirable enough in its way, of course, but you see it's a bit self-defeating in the end, isn't it? Because I mean it doesn't bring the suffering of the world to an end, does it, if we just decide to remove ourselves from it? And there are future generations to think about, you see. That's basically our position on that, anyway. So in the end that means that it does remain a crime to kill yourself or other people without our permission. We turn a blind eye a lot of the time, you know, particularly where servants and foreigners are involved, but we do have to be realistic, and there isn't really anything much we could do about that anyway, is there, even if we wanted to? Well. In any case, once you accept this basic idea that there are two components to suffering, what we call the tears and the pain, then that leads you on to the idea that there are different levels of suffering too. It's the spiritual suffering – the pain itself – that we basically think of as the purest kind there is, and so the tears, then, are only just the physical consequences of that spiritual condition. But there are other levels apart from these basic ones, ideas that we have developed over the years, you know. Like priestly suffering, for instance. We suffer by not suffering, you see, that's the thing. We deny ourselves the satisfaction of suffering in our own persons, so as to allow us the deeper satisfaction of knowing that this enables us to cause greater suffering to others. It's a great sacrifice we make, from a theoretical point of view that is. And that leads us naturally to the concept of *material suffering*. We conceive this as the next sort of level, below the priestly sacrifice. So first of all there is spiritual suffering – that is, the

actual pain – and the tears, the physical consequences, whatever they might be, are just the consequences of that. So that could be, well, tears of course, or a physical disease, or something direct like that. But after that we say that there is *material* suffering, and that's not quite the same thing. What we say, actually, is that since people love especially wealth and fine things, then, particularly if they are very wealthy, we can help them to suffer by helping them to give up some of their wealth. And the richer they are, then of course the more it hurts them. And since their suffering is the greater, it is only natural and right that in such cases we should not require any other, more direct form of suffering from them. And that's another case, you see, of how we have to adjust ourselves to what you could call the practical requirements of the situation. What's that you say? No, no, of course not. Not at all. The suffering of the rich, if that's really how you want to put it, is quite a different thing from priestly suffering. A different sort of thing altogether. They suffer by means of gifts, you see. It's quite a different sort of thing. Oh yes – and actually, over there, that's the House of Suffering for the rich people. Yes. That big marble building with the sloping roof. It's for what we call the sacrifice by proxy. As you know, every family has to register all its children with us, so that we can select the ones we need for all the sacrifices. But if the parents have been suffering by gifts, then when it comes to their turn to give up their children we say that they have acquired the right to appoint a proxy. The children still have to come for purification, but what that means in reality is that they spend a week in the House of Suffering. It's become a sort of social event, actually. The parents like to come along and watch, especially when it's time for the actual sacrifice. What? Oh, no. We still have to have a sacrifice, of course. So what we do is to tell them they have to supply a replacement. A servant or someone like that usually, or of course they can just buy someone specially if they want. But usually it's considered good taste to sacrifice someone associated with the family in some way. The child of one of the servants or something. And this isn't actually a legal requirement or anything, but there's a sort of tradition that if they want, they can perform the sacrifice themselves; and, well, they usually like to make it into a sort of party. We don't really encourage it, but, you know, if they want to, then we do have the House of Suffering there for that purpose. It's all pretty luxurious, actually. But you'll be seeing all that later. What? Oh, yes. Yes. Very expensive. Now: what else is there you should know about? Ah yes. That long low building over there is called the House of Records, and that's where we'll be starting you off for a year or two. Well, actually it could even be longer than that, but don't worry; it's only if we all decide it's the right thing for you. Some people just sort of naturally take to it. Our oldest Records man must be, what, well he must be well over seventy now, and he's been with us an awfully long time. Started out as a young man like you. But he's perfectly content with it, you see, that's the thing, and we need people who have a sort of natural talent like that. It's writing mostly, you know. What? Oh. Oh, yes. I see. Really! Well, well. How funny. Oh yes. Of course. Absolutely. I'll explain it, then. Now I suppose you've at least seen some, haven't you? Look, there's some. Those funny marks. That's it. Yes. Of course you have. Well, you see, it's a sort of symbolic system that we have. They're all like little pictures, you see, and so what you have to learn to do is to recognize what all the pictures mean. You'll get the hang of it. But the thing is, that if no-one explains it to you, then you're never going to be able to work it out. So that makes it very useful for us, you see. So for instance, what it says over there, on the wall, is "I am the shadow of a shadow of a shadow, and my blood is nothing but a teardrop". Just a sort of reminder, you know. I don't know exactly why it's there, actually, but there we are. But anyway, if you look at it, then you see at the end there's that thing that looks like a teardrop – got it? – well, that means "teardrop". But that's an unusually simple example. It's just because it's one of the oldest signs we have that still survives. We have a few very old records, using the simplest kind of writing you can imagine, and it's all made up of these simple signs like that one. Hand, head, eye, foot, that sort of thing. But over the years, you see, it's all been developed into a much more complicated sort of system. Don't worry about it now, though. You don't have to understand it all in one go. You'll pick it up. What? No. Not really. Yes! I see. No, that's just a sort of popular misconception, I'm afraid.

Magical signs made by spirits! Of course not. Yes, yes. We know all about that. Yes. Well, the thing is, we don't actually go out of our way to discourage that sort of thing. No. I mean people do demand some sort of explanation. And since we're not going to tell them the truth, then we have to let them think something about it all, don't we? But anyway, as I said, it all goes on in there. The House of Records. Now, I might as well tell you what it is that you'll be doing to start with. What we basically have is these lists. Lists of everything. Everything there is that might conceivably one day be of any use to us. So every baby that's born, for instance, has to come to us for inspection, as you know, and so we record its name, its parents' names, what colour it is, what colour its eyes are, all that sort of thing. And of course if there are any abnormalities or anything, well, then actually we have a whole special section that deals with it. There's a whole body of law, you see, dealing with monstrosities and anomalies of nature. Eclipses, earthquakes, comets: all that sort of thing. What's that? Oh, the law? Yes, yes. Of course. All written down, you see. Yes. But your father was a judge, wasn't he? Oh. Oh I see. No. Your uncle. Still, I suppose you must have had some sort of . . . Really. Yes. I see. Just a sort of general idea, then. Of course. That's right. All written down. And, well, between you and me, a lot of it is just about impossible to understand, even for us. Yes. It's in the old writing, you see. Yes. But the thing is, since no-one else can understand it at all, then basically they just have to accept whatever interpretation we come up with, don't they? And of course there are sometimes some practical considerations. I'm trying to think of an example for you . . . Oh yes. There was that case with the fruit trees. Now, fruit, as I expect you know, is deemed to be a material manifestation of the tears of Amuwapi. Yes, it is strange, isn't it? But there we are. So because all fruit naturally belongs to the temple and to us, we distribute it from here and keep the change, as it were. However, there was a finding, oh, a long time ago, that although fruit belongs to the material world, the trees themselves, being living things, are from a legal point of view part of what we call the thousand things, and therefore in a technical sense free independent beings. This is just legal jargon, you understand. I mean a slave is a free independent being from the legal point of view too, for instance. Anyway, what it basically means is that as free independent beings, trees, including fruit trees, can be bought and sold in the normal way – like slaves, you see. Now, about, what was it, oh, about six or seven months ago it must have been we had a case where one of our most generous sufferers – Gul-shliop, actually, you're sure to run across him. Very rich. Anyway, he discovered that there was a whole hillside of wild plum trees that he simply didn't know about, just at the edge of his estate. And there was rather a delicate legal question, you see, because there was actually a family of goat-herds living right there on that hillside, and they claimed, when it came to court, firstly that they had always lived there, which was true as far as anyone could tell, and secondly – and this was the difficult part of it – that not only had they always lived there, but also they had always collected up every last one of the plums that fell to the ground each year, and brought them here to the temple as tribute. And as I said, we do keep very careful records of everything like that, and when we checked up, we found that that seemed to be true as well! They had been coming along every year for hundreds of years with their baskets of wild plums for the temple, and no-one had ever given it a second thought. But that was before this fashion for plum wine, you see. So it was all quite a difficult matter. So, what did we do? Well, it all took quite a bit of head-scratching, let me tell you, but in the end it was ruled that the goat-herds had been in the right to collect all the plums each year, and indeed this was deemed to be their sacred duty in this case. But when it came to the trees, well, it was quite a different matter. It was decided that by setting up a home right there on the hillside among the trees, the family had in effect been making what amounted to a legal claim to own the trees for all that time. Yes, I'm afraid so. Well, they protested, of course, as you can imagine, that that had never been their intention, and the court did concede this, but of course we can't make exceptions on the basis of ignorance of the law. That would be a most dangerous principle to allow. And, well, blasphemous ownership is a most serious charge at the best of times; but you see the court's investigation of the case had revealed that the crime had been going on for literally hundreds of years, with the whole family openly claiming ownership of the trees for all that time. I don't remember exactly how long they said it had all been going on. But of course you can see the point, can't you? Only the rich may own. It's one of our most basic legal principles. So, anyway, in the end it all turned out more or less OK. Gul-shliop was awarded the guardianship of the trees in perpetuity, which means of course that he now has legal discretion over what to do with the fruit; and I mean it's not entirely inconceivable, is it, that he might in his wisdom decide that Amuwapi will be best served if the fruit is converted into some other sort of worship. Plum wine for instance. No. No. What? Oh, yes. The family. Well, they got what they deserved, of course. Quite shocking, really. Hundreds of years it had all been going on! The father was given for death by breaking, as you can imagine, and we used the brothers for the sacrifices, I forget which ones exactly. The women were divided between the temple and Gul-shliop's estate. Yes, actually, come to think of it, there's one of them in particular up in the bath-house that's definitely worth saying hello to! I tell you what: why don't we go over there and I'll introduce you. Really quite a lovely little thing. All right? Fine. Now you're rested. And anyway, I expect you'll want a little while to sort of think things over. But the main thing is, Don't Worry! You'll be fine. Anyway, shall we . . . ? Yes, this way. Careful! That's it. You have to be careful not to slip. It's all the blood, you see. They scrub it all away, but it's funny really, it still seems to leave a sort of slime or something behind. Smells a bit funny, too. But anyway . . .

TEAR OF AMUWAPI WITH A HAND OFFERING SACRIFICE.

Bronze, Shang Dynasty. (Léon Wieger, S.J., *Chinese Characters. Their origin, etymology, history, classification, and signification. A thorough study from Chinese documents.* Translated into English by L. Davrout, S. J., 2nd edition, Catholic Mission Press, 1927, enlarged and revised according to the 4th French edition. Paragon Book Reprint Corp., New York, 1965)

Rama Wijaya ascended the mountain of the ape king. Hanoman Duta saw them coming and came forward to welcome them. Rama Wijaya narrated the story of his beautiful wife Shinta's abduction by Prabu Rahwana, the ruler of Alengkadiraja, and spoke of his determination to regain her.

The Adventures of the Ape Envoy Hanoman Duta
Semarang, Central Java, 1996

THE SULTAN AND THE MAN IN RAGS

One day the Sultan said, "Now I am very lonely."

"Then I will send for the women from the harem!" said the Keeper of the Sultan's Women.

"Oh, no!" said the Sultan. "Not the women from the harem!"

"Then I will send for your hawks and hounds!" said the Keeper of the Hawks and Hounds.

"Oh, no!" said the Sultan. "Not the hawks and hounds!"

"Then I will send for your gold and jewels!" said the Keeper of the Gold and Jewels.

"Oh, no!" said the Sultan. "For it is jewels and gold and hawks and hounds and the women from the harem that have made me so lonely in the first place."

And the Keeper of the Sultan's Women, and the Keeper of the Hounds and Hawks, and the Keeper of the Sultan's Treasure, all shook their heads in wonder. They had never known the Sultan to speak like this – and in the end they sent for the Sultan's doctor, for they were afraid, you see, that the Sultan was gravely ill.

"He is bewitched!" said the Keeper of the Hawks and Hounds.

"He is not himself!" said the Keeper of the Treasure.

"He is mad!" said the Keeper of the Women. They all looked at him. "Oh yes," he said sadly. "Quite mad." And they all shook their heads very seriously.

"Well," said the Sultan's doctor, who was an old, old man, with a long grey beard, "I had better take a look at him."

"Now," he said, when he had been admitted to the Sultan's presence, "What seems to be the matter?" But the Sultan just looked at him contemptuously.

"You are an old fool and a charlatan," he said, in a very direct sort of voice, and the Keepers of the Hawks and Hounds and Women and Jewels and Gold (who were hiding behind a curtain) all shook their heads. "There is nothing at all the matter with me, except that I am very lonely, as I have already said, I think."

"Ah," said the Doctor, stroking his beard and trying to sound wise. "Yes." He looked at the Sultan with narrowed, professional eyes. "Tell me, how have you been sleeping?"

"Guards!" shouted the Sultan. "Take this idiot away and have him thrown to the crocodiles and vultures!"

"Oh, no!" said the Doctor, falling to his knees.

"Oh, yes!" said the Sultan. "For I have had enough of you. The whole pack of you. I should have done this a long time ago. And what's more, as I think I may have mentioned, I feel very lonely. Guards! Where are they?"

But the Keeper of the Treasure and the Keeper of the Women and the Keeper of the Hounds and Hawks had all rushed out to tell the guards that His Supreme Highness was not feeling quite himself.

The Sultan paced around angrily in his chamber, kicking his feet in their jewelled slippers at the chamber's thick carpets and soft cushions. The Doctor cowered, with lowered eyes and shaking hands. But where were the guards?

"Guards!" shouted the Sultan again, but it was only because he felt like shouting. He had realized that they were not going to come. "Idiot!" he said bitterly to the Doctor as he passed him. "Miserable old fool!"

After a time, a man dressed in rags entered the Sultan's apartment. He was wiping his hands on his filthy old trousers, and looking around at everything very nervously. The Sultan considered him with some interest. It was not often that he saw a poor person from close up.

"Who are you?" he said.

"I am the Keeper of the Vultures and Crocodiles, may it please your Excellency," said the man.

"The Keeper of the Vultures and Crocodiles?" repeated the Sultan. "But that's splendid! I didn't realize that there was such a position."

"Oh yes," said the man. He looked at the Sultan shrewdly. "In fact, it's hereditary."

"Hereditary?" said the Sultan. "That's strange. Tell me, how did your forebears acquire this honour? Did they render some extraordinary service to one of our ancestors or something?" The man looked around carefully and leaned forward to speak very privately.

"Actually, your Excellency, it's more in the nature of a punishment."

"Ah."

"But we have always maintained our innocence, you know."

"Quite so," said the Sultan, vaguely; but now he was beginning to lose interest. "Well, anyway, now that you are here, I suppose you had better sit down."

"Thanks, your Excellency," said the man, sitting down carefully on the edge of a large pink cushion. The Sultan draped himself more grandly over an adjacent sofa and considered the man some more. It really was quite remarkable how dirty and ragged he was.

"And what is it that I can do for you exactly?" he asked after a while.

"It's about his Excellency there," said the man, indicating the terrified Doctor with a nod of his head.

"Oh," said the Sultan, in a disappointed sort of voice. "What about him?"

"Well, you see, it's like this. They told me . . . " But the Sultan had interrupted him by holding up an imperious finger.

"They?"

"Ah. Yes." The man looked at the floor.

"Let me guess. You wouldn't by any chance be referring to the accomplices and partners in crime of this useless wretch, would you?"

"Well . . . " The man looked really quite frightened now.

"Namely, the Keepers of my Women and Treasure and Hounds and Hawks," said the Sultan. "Or would you?"

"I suppose they were sort of involved a bit," admitted the man eventually.

"I thought as much. Well get on with it then. What did they tell you to say?" He tried to sound angry and contemptuous at the same time, but it just sounded tired; and he reached out his foot to give the Doctor a kick in the behind, to let him know he hadn't forgotten him.

"It's against the regulations," the man said quickly.

"What?" said the Sultan, in a voice of thunder.

"Yes. That's what they said I had to tell you. Completely against all palace traditions, rules, and as I say also regulations to feed senior palace officials to the vultures and crocodiles. No precedent for it, you see." The Sultan looked at him sternly. "Can't be done," the man finished lamely.

"I see," said the Sultan, considering. He had to admit that he had never tried it before. "Who can I have thrown to the crocodiles and vultures, then?"

"Oh, anyone," said the man. "Just no palace officials, that's all. Sorry."

"Oh, it's not your fault," said the Sultan. He stood up and paced around, thinking about it; and he kicked the Doctor in the behind again to demonstrate that he still wasn't happy about how things were going.

"I'm not very happy, you know," he said.

"I know," said the man. "I mean, I can see that. Er . . . "

"Well?"

"Well, I was just wondering . . . I don't suppose there's anything I can do, is there? Apart from throwing his Excellency there to the vultures and crocodiles, I mean." The Sultan looked at him pessimistically.

"Oh, get out," he said suddenly, kicking the Doctor again as hard as he could. But the man could see that the Sultan wasn't talking to him; and as the Doctor limped out, the man settled himself a little more comfortably on his cushion. He tried to look sympathetic.

"The thing is," said the Sultan, when they were alone, "I feel terribly, terribly lonely."

"That's terrible," said the man.

"I know."

"Have you tried alcohol?" said the man, thinking about it.

"What?"

"Alcohol. Very good for loneliness."

"Really?"

"Oh yes. Loneliness, heartache, all that sort of thing. I'm surprised you haven't . . . "

"Oh, well, I know what it does, of course, in a general sort of way; it's just that, well, I hope you won't be offended, but you see it's always seemed . . . well, a bit sort of *vulgar*."

"I'd never really looked at it like that, your Excellency."

"No. Well I'm afraid it has always had that sort of connotation. But tell me, do you . . . Well, I mean . . . "

"Do I drink the stuff?"

"Yes."

"Oh, like a fish, your Excellency."

"And . . . well, and you'd recommend it, would you? For loneliness?"

"I'd say you've got nothing to lose."

And soon the Sultan and the Keeper of the Vultures and Crocodiles were the best of friends. It just so happened that the man in rags had several bottles of strong drink concealed about his person. The Sultan was a little bit hesitant as they drank the first bottle, but by the time they got on to the third one, he knew he was doing the right thing.

"I must say, you really are a splendid fellow," he said, clapping the Keeper of the Crocodiles and Vultures on the back. "But tell me, I don't mean to pry, you know, but well, how much do they pay you, actually, for this post of yours? I mean, forgive me, but you don't look very *rich*, actually."

"Pay?" said the man.

"Well, yes, I mean surely they must pay you *something* . . . "

"Not really."

"But that's terrible!"

"I know."

"But... Why do you do it, then?"

"What do you mean?"

"Well... a man with your talents..." But the man laughed bitterly. He looked carefully around again, as if he didn't want anyone else to hear what he had to say.

"Well, it's more in the nature of a *sentence*, actually, your Excellency." The Sultan looked puzzled.

"But... What have you done, then, exactly?"

"No, no, I told you. It's hereditary. Cheers."

"Cheers," said the Sultan absent-mindedly. He was trying hard to understand. Fortunately, the man was relaxing a bit now, and getting more talkative. He leaned forward to explain his predicament.

"I come from a long line of story-tellers," he said.

"Oh," said the Sultan. "That's good."

"Oh no," said the man, with a bitter laugh, "It's not good at all. You see, my great-great-grandfather, may Allah protect and save him, once composed a story which was, so they say, misinterpreted in some circles as an attack on the Sultanate."

"No!"

"Yes." They both looked serious at this striking thought. "But, as I think I may have said, we have always maintained that the old boy was innocent. You can't trust critics, you know."

"Really?"

"Take it from me. Anyway, ever since then, in an attempt to silence us, and also so as to expose us to the ridicule and contempt of the populace, we have to devote ourselves to the upkeep of the palace vultures and crocodiles, which is a pretty depressing task, by the way. Revolting. But there you are. Cheers." And he drank some more of the alcohol.

"So I suppose you still have some opportunities to exercise your profession, then?" said the Sultan, trying to cheer him up.

"In a manner of speaking. My forebears, you know, used to squat in the most prestigious tents available. But yes, I do still entertain a handful of village illiterates every now and again. Small boys, mainly." And they both drank sombrely at the thought of how low the man had fallen. The Sultan's mind seemed to be working a lot more slowly than usual for some reason, and so it took him some time to formulate the next, obvious question.

"I don't suppose you could think of an appropriate story to tell me right now, could you?" The man thought about it.

"I don't really know. What sort of theme would most delight your Excellency?"

"Well," said the Sultan, and a lump came to his throat and a tear to his eye as he thought about it. "I must say that I have been rather preoccupied lately with the idea of loneliness. Did I tell you that? I don't remember."

"You may have mentioned something along those lines, I think," said the man. He drank deeply. "Perhaps I can think of something . . . Ah yes! I know the very thing."

"Oh, good!"

"Yes," said the man. "In honour of this great occasion" (and now he seemed to be getting a bit emotional himself) "I think I will repeat one of the tales that has been passed down from mouth to mouth, as we say, through long long centuries, from the time of our illustrious ancestor Ursalim himself. Down long, long lines of fathers and sons, through the rise and fall of great empires, and down to me."

"Golly," said the Sultan. But the Keeper of the Palace Vultures and Crocodiles was getting into character now, and he held up a finger for silence.

"It is a story which Ursalim, they say, learned from the ancient tales, which still flowed uncorrupted in his days. Let us fill our glasses."

"Good idea." But first they had to empty them, of course.

"Now this story, you know, concerns a catfish, and is called *The Catfish and the Peacock*."

And the Sultan smiled expectantly.

THE CATFISH AND THE PEACOCK

Once there was a catfish, who was really very lonely. All day long he searched and searched, in every pond and river and lake he could find, and when the birds and animals he met asked him what it was that he was searching for, he would answer them wearily, "It is Love. It is nothing but Love that I am searching for like this."

There was an eagle who laughed out loud at the catfish and his search.

"It is ridiculous!" said the eagle. "That is no way to search for anything! Why, when I want to search for something, then I fly so high in the sky that I see all the world spread out below me like a cloth on a table. And then I can see whatever there is to be seen."

"Tell me," said the catfish, "Since you are so wise; what do you find when you search like that?"

"Oh, rats, mice, that sort of thing," said the eagle modestly. "Rabbits sometimes. You know."

"But I am not searching for rats or mice, you see," said the catfish politely. "Or rabbits." And with that he continued on his way.

Sometimes, when the water was particularly muddy and murky, the catfish couldn't see where he was going at all, and he just had to trust to luck that he was still heading in the right direction. It wasn't really a very good system, though, as he often thought to himself. One day he was making his way down a particularly obscure-seeming little ditch when he suddenly bumped his head against a strange, upside-down sort of thing. Pink, it was. He peered at it with his old grey eyes and tried to make out what it was.

"Hello," it said.

"Hello," said the catfish.

"Why are you looking at me like that?"

"I'm sorry. I don't mean to be rude. It's just that I've never come across anyone like you. There's something very strange about you, you know."

"Really?"

"Really. You seem to be all upside-down or something."

"Oh, yes. I'm a flamingo, you see."

"What?" But the flamingo pulled its head out of the water and stood up straight to talk to the catfish.

"I'm a flamingo."

"Oh! That's better."

"Better for you, I suppose."

"What do you mean?"

"Well, I mean, I suppose it's better for you, that's all. But you see it's all very confusing for me if I have to stand up straight like this. All the blood sort of rushes to my legs. It's very uncomfortable."

"I'm sorry to hear that."

"Oh, it's not your fault. But what's really confusing is that it makes everything seem sort of upside-down. It's difficult to explain."

"I think I see what you mean," said the catfish.

"Really? Well that's unusual. All the other birds think I'm an idiot." And the flamingo let fall a small pink flamingo tear. "They say that I see everything all upside-down and topsy-turvy, you see. They all laugh at me."

"Oh, don't worry about that," said the catfish. "I met an eagle a while ago, and he laughed at me, too."

"Oh yes. I know all about the eagle," said the flamingo wearily. "But he's not the worst, you know. Far from it. You just have to learn to put up with it, that's all. But anyway, what is it you're doing down there exactly?"

"I am searching for Love," said the catfish. "I don't suppose you have any idea where I might find it?"

"Love?" And the flamingo stood on one leg to think about it.

"Does that help?" said the catfish.

"Well, yes, it does help a bit," said the flamingo. "At least this way the blood

only rushes into one leg at a time. Now, let me see . . . *Love*, you say?"

"That's it," said the catfish. "Love."

"Hmm. I think I might have heard of something like that."

"Really?"

"But I'm not sure. I am a very stupid bird, I'm afraid."

"Oh, no! Come, come."

"Oh yes. I'm afraid I am. Ask anyone. But I'd like to help you. Can you describe it?"

"Not really," admitted the catfish.

"Well, that's not really very helpful, is it? I mean, even if I had seen it somewhere hereabouts, I still might not be able to tell you. Don't you know anything about it at all?"

"Not much, I'm afraid," said the catfish. "But I expect I'll know when I find it."

"Well that must be a comfort, I suppose," said the flamingo sympathetically.

"I'd better just keep looking, then," said the catfish.

"I suppose so," said the flamingo. "Only . . . "

"Yes?"

"Only I suppose there is one thing you could try."

"What's that?"

"Well, as I said, I am universally recognized to be a particularly stupid bird."

"Surely not."

"Oh yes. I'm afraid so. And as for my advice, it is generally taken to be completely worthless. But there is one particular bird who is quite famous for his all-seeing wisdom and encyclopaedic general knowledge. Perhaps you could go and ask him what he thinks about it. Only you'll have to wait until it gets dark, because he only comes out at night."

"Oh, that's all right. I can search around on my own for a bit till then. But tell me, what is his name, this wise and knowledgeable bird of which you speak?"

"His name is Owl."

"Owl," repeated the catfish carefully. "Well, that's easy enough. And how will

I recognize him?"

"Can you see in the dark?"

"Not really."

"Well in that case you'll just have to listen out for his voice. Too wit to woo is what he chiefly says."

"Too wit to woo?"

"Exactly. And now, if you don't mind, all this upside down conversation is really making my head spin."

"I won't keep you any longer, then. But I shall certainly look out for your friend the owl."

"Oh, he's not exactly my friend," said the flamingo, stretching out his neck and plunging his head back into the water in relief that the conversation was over at last. "In fact, he thinks I'm an idiot." The catfish nearly said something comforting, but then he noticed the strangest thing. When the flamingo was standing up, he really looked quite miserable; but now that he was looking at everything upside-down again, it suddenly seemed as if he had a smile of perfect upside-down contentment on his beak: and so the catfish decided he would just leave him to get on with it.

"Goodbye," he said. "And thank you."

"And good luck!" said the flamingo. "Don't mention it."

Well, the catfish searched and searched all the rest of that day, but as usual he found no trace of what he was searching for. And when the evening came, he listened very attentively for the sound of the owl; and sure enough, after a while he heard a far-off voice calling out in the darkness.

"Too wit to woo! Too wit to woo!"

"Hello!" called the catfish, as loudly as he could. "Hello! Mr Owl!"

"Too wit to woo!" came the voice again, but much closer this time, and in a minute a dark mysterious shape flapped over the ditch and settled itself in the branch of a tree.

"Too wit to woo!" said the owl. "What do you want?"

"Good evening," said the catfish. "I have been looking for you."

"Oh yes," said the owl. "Of course you have. I knew that all along."

"Well why did you ask me what I wanted, then?"

"Never mind that," said the owl, a little crossly. "But hurry up and tell me what you want exactly. I haven't got all night, you know."

"Well!" thought the catfish. "This owl is a rude and ungracious sort of creature!" But of course he was too polite to say so. Instead, he said, "Yes of course. The thing is, I was talking to a flamingo . . . "

"Too wit to woo!" interrupted the owl. "That idiot! Always sees everything upside-down, you know."

"Yes," said the catfish carefully. "I know."

"Well if you already know, then why are you bothering me about it? Really!" And the owl flapped his wings crossly. "I'm very busy, you know."

"Actually, there was another matter," said the catfish quickly. "You see, I am searching for Love."

"Love?" said the owl incredulously.

"Love," said the catfish. "And the flamingo thought you might have some suggestions. Seeing as you are so wise and intelligent."

"Quite so," said the owl, evidently pleased at this turn in the conversation. "Quite so indeed. Hmm." He fell silent. After a while, the catfish coughed politely, but the owl flapped his wings angrily. "Too wit to woo! Can't you see I'm thinking?"

"I'm afraid I can't see very well in the dark," said the catfish apologetically.

"Well I know that, of course. What do you take me for, eh? But anyway, listen, I've been thinking about your problem, and I believe I have an answer for you."

"Really? Oh, good!" said the catfish.

"Well I don't know about that," said the owl. "No good will come of it, mark my words. Love! It is ridiculous. And the first thing you have to understand is that we reasonable creatures don't waste our time on that sort of nonsense."

"Oh."

"We have more important matters to think about, let me tell you, such as rats and mice and that sort of thing."

"Rabbits," said the catfish gloomily.

"Exactly. But I do know of one creature that is foolish enough to take an interest in such things."

"Oh! What is his name?" said the catfish eagerly.

"He is called the peacock."

"I have never heard of such a creature."

"That is because he lives in the far-off land of Persia. But I warn you, he really is a singularly foolish bird."

"Well, never mind," said the catfish, thinking secretly of his friend the flamingo. "Sometimes even foolish creatures have their uses, you know."

"Well I don't know about that, too wit to woo!" said the owl disagreeably.

"How will I recognize him?" said the catfish, so as to change the subject.

"Oh, he has a most unpleasant squawk. A sort of loud and high-pitched screeching noise. You will recognize him by that. Oh yes, and he has a long and ridiculous tail, too."

"And where does he live exactly? In Persia, you say?"

"Yes, yes, that's right. Away in far-off Persia. That's where he lives. In a special magic garden, they say, with walls of silver and gold."

"Oh!" said the catfish, impressed.

"Yes. And there is a magic river running through the garden, they say, and the peacock goes to drink there every day around lunchtime. So that's where you will find him." The catfish thought about this.

"And where, please, is Persia, exactly?"

"Well really!" said the owl crossly. "Too wit to woo! I'm not a tourist information service, you know!" And with that, he flapped off again into the night, leaving the catfish to find his way to Persia all by himself.

Well, it took the catfish many a long year to find his way to the far-off land of Persia. But at least he felt he had something to aim at now. And when he asked the creatures he met if they knew which way it was to Persia, they would at least be able to give him some kind of answer. "This way," one might say, or "That way." But of course the problem was that usually they didn't really know, and so he wasted many a long journey going in completely the wrong direction. But eventually he did manage to arrive in the magical land of Persia, after travelling through who knows how many nameless seas and rivers and ditches and whatnot. And once he was in Persia, it was a relatively simple matter to find the magic garden with its walls of silver and gold. For the garden, he discovered, was famous throughout the whole land of Persia, where it was known as the Garden of Solitude. It belonged, they said, to a great and powerful wizard, who had decided to live there all alone, with only the rarest and most beautiful things in the world for company. And when the catfish reached the garden, he understood why it was called the Garden of Solitude. For there was no gate or doorway or other entrance. The walls of silver and gold went all the way around without a break. The catfish was able to ascertain this quite clearly, because there was a muddy moat which went all the way around the outside of the walls, and he had been able to find his way into this moat. But there was no connecting passage or channel from the moat to the inside of the garden either; and to add to his frustration at not being able to get in, he could hear, from the inside of the garden, a sort of screeching sound, that he supposed was the "squawking" the owl had told him about. The peacock! It was all very depressing.

He was swimming sluggishly around the walls, for what seemed like the hundredth or the thousandth time, when (to his great astonishment) a clear little voice called out to him.

"Hey, you!" it said. "Stop that, will you? It's making me quite dizzy." The catfish stopped dead and looked around to see who had spoken to him. He looked and looked, but couldn't for the life of him work out where the voice could have come from.

"That's better," said the voice. "Going round and round like that won't do you any good at all, you know. You have to know the magic spell." This time the catfish looked even more carefully, and he thought he could see two eyes looking back at him from the wall; and suddenly *plop!* a beautiful little gold and silver frog detached itself from the wall where it had been sitting and watching, and jumped into the moat. It swam gracefully up to the catfish and introduced itself.

"Hello," it said. "I Make No Promises."

"What?" said the catfish, confused.

"That's my name. I Make No Promises. What's your name?"

"I don't know," said the catfish. "I don't think I have a name."

"Well frankly you're better off without one. Mine has been nothing but a torment I can assure you. But anyway, I'm the wallkeeper."

"What's a wallkeeper?"

"Well," explained I Make No Promises patiently, "If we had a door then I'd be the doorkeeper, you see, only we don't. We just have a wall, as you've no doubt realized. So that makes me the wallkeeper, doesn't it?"

"I see," said the catfish, thinking about it. "So you mean you deal with visitors, then?"

"In a manner of speaking," said I Make No Promises.

"What do you mean?"

"Well, I mean that actually there aren't really exactly what you would call *visitors*. I wouldn't want to get your hopes up. It's not called the Garden of Solitude for nothing, you know."

"I see," said the catfish gloomily.

"But still," said I Make No Promises, "Why don't you tell me what it is you're trying to achieve here? I suppose we might possibly be able to come to some sort of understanding. Who knows?"

"I am searching for Love," said the catfish.

"Love?" I Make No Promises sounded sceptical.

"Love. And I spoke to a wise and intelligent creature called an owl, and the owl told me that I should come to Persia and seek out the bird called the peacock, who might be able to advise me on this matter. And if I am not deceived, that cry we sometimes hear is in fact nothing but the cry of the peacock himself. Or am I mistaken?"

"Not at all," admitted I Make No Promises. "That's him all right. But I really should warn you, the peacock is a particularly foolish creature."

"So I understand. But anyway . . . "

"Yes. Yes, I see the point. Look, I tell you what I'll do. Now, as you know, the Boss doesn't normally encourage visitors. Not nohow. But seeing as how you've come all this way, and seeing as how you're not planning to upset the Boss with any impertinent enquiries or requests for money or military assistance or anything like that . . . "

"Oh, not at all!" said the catfish. "Nothing like that, I assure you!"

"Well in that case I'll see what I can do. Just you wait here for a bit."

"Oh, thank you!" said the catfish joyfully.

"Don't thank me yet. Remember: I make no promises." And with that he was off. He jumped back on to the wall and just seemed to disappear.

The catfish waited and waited. The night fell, and still I Make No Promises didn't return; and the catfish, tired of waiting, started to swim sluggishly round and round again. He was still swimming around when the morning came.

"Oh, stop that, can't you!" came the voice again, eventually, and the catfish stopped and stared around again; but look as he might, he still couldn't pick out I Make No Promises from the wall he was sitting on: not until I Make No Promises jumped *plop!* into the water again to swim alongside the catfish.

"You are a most impatient creature, aren't you?" he said.

"I suppose it depends what you're used to," said the catfish diplomatically.

"Perhaps. Anyway, listen, I've talked it over with the Boss . . . "

"And?"

"Now just calm down a bit. There's no point getting all excited. The Boss says that basically it's OK."

"Really? Oh good!"

"Well maybe. As I think I may have already said, I make no promises. I don't know exactly what you expect to get out of the peacock, but it's only fair to warn you: he really is a most foolish bird. But anyway, if you're sure you've made up your mind to go through with this . . . "

"Oh yes! I want it more than anything!"

"Then the Boss says that he's prepared to allow you one short interview with the peacock. It's an unusual concession, you know, so I hope you're suitably impressed."

"Oh yes! I'm deeply honoured. Grateful, too."

"Hmm. But anyway, the thing is, there is one condition."

"What's that?" But the catfish was too excited to be worried.

"Well, the Boss does sometimes get a bit lonely sitting all alone in his Garden of Solitude and not having any contact with the outside world, which is basically repellent in his eyes, I should explain. But I'm sure you understand that."

"Absolutely," said the catfish – though actually he wasn't sure exactly what it was that he was supposed to understand.

"So what he'd like in return for this extraordinary privilege of your being allowed to discuss your search for Love with the peacock is a few moments of distraction and entertainment."

"How do you mean, exactly?"

"Well, it's like this," said I Make No Promises, choosing his words with some care. "Normally, you see, the Boss likes to surround himself with rare and beautiful creatures such as myself. The peacock, for instance, whom you are so eager to interview, falls into this category too. Now, I'm sure you have many virtues . . . "

"Thank you," said the catfish.

"But frankly, beauty ain't one of them. Actually, you look like a slug with fins on. Facts is facts."

"I suppose you're right," said the catfish, who hadn't ever really thought about this aspect of things before.

"Well, seeing as how these are the basic conditions, then, the Boss, having considered it all very carefully and from every possible angle, has decided that seeing as how you aren't much good from the point of view of ornamentation, basically what he's going to require from you in return for this extraordinary concession on his part is a story."

"What?"

"You heard. Think you can manage it?"

"Oh yes," said the catfish. "I can manage that all right."

"Is it a deal, then?" said I Make No Promises.

"It's a deal," said the catfish. And suddenly there was a great shimmering and clanging and rushing of air, and the scene they were in seemed to turn itself completely inside-out. The walls stayed the same, more or less, but now they were somehow on the inside, in the garden, and the air was filled with beautiful scents and sounds. Strange flowers and trees were all around, and lynxes and avocets prowled and stalked among the delicate and colourful plants.

"Golly," said the catfish. The shallow muddy moat, too, had somehow also been transformed; and now the catfish found himself in the sparkling water of a magic river, that came from nowhere and went nowhere. The water bubbled and sprang over well-proportioned waterfalls and into elegant little pools and thoughtful brooks and even an exuberant fountain or two. But if all these things made the catfish rub his eyes, the change in I Make No Promises could have made a more excitable creature than the catfish jump out of its skin in shock and astonishment: for I Make No Promises had leapt lightly to the bank as all the transformation had started, and the little gold and silver frog that had left the water now arrived on the mossy bank as a tall and serious-looking man, dressed in a flowing robe of gold and silver.

"It . . . it's you!" said the catfish, not very coherently.

"Yes. Sorry about the little deception. Can't be too careful."

"No," said the catfish, though actually he didn't know exactly what it was that you couldn't be too careful about. The wizard snapped his fingers, and a large throne appeared, on which he sat himself easily down. A glass of something fizzy appeared in his hand, and he sipped at it thoughtfully. "You know, there's something funny about this water." said the catfish, splashing about in it a little. "I've never known a river like this one; and I've been in a lot of rivers."

"It is a river of tears," said the wizard.

"Oh," said the catfish. "I see."

"Now, what about that story?"

"Oh yes," said the catfish, pulling himself together.

"Well, I haven't got all day, you know." But actually the catfish didn't believe him.

"No," he said, hypocritically.

"What kind of story do you propose to tell me?" said the wizard.

"Oh, that's easy," said the catfish, "For there is only one story I know."

"And does it have a name, this story of yours?"

"Oh certainly. The name of the story is *Amuwapi at the Beginning of the World*."

"Well I should certainly like to hear it. Proceed." So the catfish took a deep breath and began.

AMUWAPI AT THE BEGINNING OF THE WORLD

Long, long ago, at the very first beginning of all the whole wide world, there was a great god, and he was all alone. Amuwapi was his name, and he was very very unhappy. In fact, he was so unhappy that all he did from morning to night was to weep great tears of unhappiness to himself. And no-one ever came to comfort him.

He wept and wept, and since there was nothing else in the world, and nowhere else for Amuwapi's tears to go, they made a great river, and that river became the great river that flows for all eternity around the edge of the world, but even so, there was nothing about it that could make Amuwapi stop his weeping.

But the world is nothing but growth and change, and after many, many years had passed, the great river that sprang from Amuwapi's tears was full of teeming life. A million brightly-coloured fish danced in its crystal depths. Dragonflies and scorpions and spiders scuttled along its edges. And last but not least, gold and silver frogs swam lazily around, leaping occasionally for dragonflies.

One day, one of these frogs (whose name was Bes, which means "I promise" in the ancient language) was running along idly when he came upon Amuwapi himself. Amuwapi was weeping and weeping, of course, and Bes just could not understand it.

"Amuwapi," he said. "Why are you weeping? Come with me and I will teach you to swim as I do in this beautiful river." But Amuwapi did not want to swim in a river made of his own tears.

"I am weeping for a reason you will never be able to understand," said Amuwapi. "But listen. If I send someone to swim with you in the river, will you promise never to bother me again?"

"Bes," said the frog. And that is how he got his name. And Amuwapi clapped his hands and made a man, who was the very first man in the whole wide world, and he called the man "my brother", and he sent him away with the frog called Bes so that he could learn how to swim in the river.

The world is nothing but difference and division; and since the great river was now in the world, it soon followed that there was something in the world that was not the river – and this is how the dry land came into being. And trees and bushes and flowers and all the plants in the whole wide world grew and blossomed there, and then the birds and animals came to live among the trees and bushes, and before long the world was full of all the thousand things. But Amuwapi could still do nothing but weep hopelessly. For he was still alone, and he still didn't know what to do about it.

Among all the creatures that ran in the forest that grew by the side of the great river, there was none so graceful or so beautiful as the golden deer called Ahtru (which means "forever" in the ancient language). Ahtru was always happy, running and dancing for joy among the forest trees. One day, she came across Amuwapi, who was weeping alone as usual, and she felt very distressed.

"Poor Amuwapi," she said. "Why are you weeping like this?"

"I am weeping for reasons you would never be able to understand," said Amuwapi. "But I do not mean for you to be unhappy too. Please, do not be so distressed."

"Then come and dance with me in the forest," said Ahtru to Amuwapi. "And I will teach you to run like the wind."

"Oh, I do not need to run like the wind," said Amuwapi (who knew that the wind and the trees and the river and the land and all the thousand things were nothing but his own tears and what had grown from them). "But if you promise that you will remember forever that you must not be alone or unhappy, then I will send someone to dance with you in the forest. So tell me, how long will you remember what I say?"

"Ahtru," said the deer. And that is how she got her name. And Amuwapi clapped his hands, and made a woman, who was the very first woman in the whole wide world, and he called the woman "my sister", and he sent her away with the deer called Ahtru so that she could learn to run like the wind in the forest. But Amuwapi was still alone, and he didn't know what he could do about it.

The world is nothing but secrets and mysteries, and every single one of all the

thousand things had some special secret thing to call its own. And even the tiny insignificant ant, that seems no more to us than a blade of grass or a drop of water, knows a great secret that is all its own. It knows how to make rules and organization and how to remember and never forget: and that is how the ants can live ten million together and never die of famine or war or pestilence. And one day there was one particular ant, whose name was Thlistra, which means "nonsense!" in the ancient language, who came upon Amuwapi, who was all alone, of course, and weeping and weeping and weeping, as usual.

"Now look here, Amuwapi," said the ant in a busy little voice. "This just won't do, you know. It won't do at all! Don't you have a job of work to do, eh? No time for all this moping about when there's work to be done, you know!" But Amuwapi just shook his head.

"You cannot understand why I am weeping," he said.

"Oh, stuff and nonsense," said the ant. "It's all a question of discipline. Just you come along with me, and I'll show you how it all operates."

"Oh, no," said Amuwapi. "I will not learn your rules and regulations. But I will send you someone who will – as long as you promise that you will leave me alone forever. For I cannot stand your rules and regulations."

"Thlistra!" said the ant, crossly. And that is how he got his name. But all the same, Amuwapi clapped his hands and made a man, and he called the man "my father", and he sent him with the ant called Thlistra to learn all about rules and regulations and organization. They headed off together into the forest along one of the ants' invisible pathways, and secretly Amuwapi was glad to see them go. But when they had gone, Amuwapi was alone again, and there was nothing for him to do but to go back to his weeping.

Well, it wasn't long before Amuwapi realized that he had made a bad mistake. His father learned all sorts of rules and regulations from Thlistra the ant, and before long he had made nets to catch the fish that swam in the great river, and he had made bows and arrows to catch all the creatures that ran in the forest, and he had made fires to devour the plants and trees and bushes, and he would have caught the wind itself and tied it up in a bag if he could have thought of a way to manage it. The frog Bes had to jump into the sky, it is said, to escape from the nets in the river where he had swum so happily since the beginning of the world; and the deer Ahtru had to run like the wind just to escape from the knives and spears and bows and arrows that Amuwapi's children, and their children, and their children's children, had learned to make to hurt her. But most of the thousand things could not escape, and Amuwapi just wept more copiously when he learned what he had done. And all his family worshipped and respected him, for they said that it was all because of him that they had their knives and spears and bows and arrows and fire and nets and all the rest of it. They built a great palace for him, and they declared that all the world belonged to him alone – but still they could not understand why it was that Amuwapi could not stop himself from weeping. And among all the thousand things, the only one that was really and truly happy was Thlistra the ant, who saw his invisible pathways spreading and spreading through all the wide world.

One day, the wise old sun decided that he could no longer stand to see Amuwapi weeping like that.

"Amuwapi!" he said. "Listen to me! I have watched you weeping since the beginning of the world."

"Yes," said Amuwapi. "I know."

"Well, now it is time for me to tell you that enough is enough. The whole wide world is filled with your children and their children and their children's children, and there is nothing you can do about it."

"I know," said Amuwapi. "You are right."

"And they see you weeping, Amuwapi. As soon as my light comes in the morning they see it; and they see it until my light is gone in the evening. And are you not ashamed?"

"Yes," said Amuwapi miserably. "Now you mention it I must say that you are right. I am ashamed to weep like this in front of them. But there is nothing I can do."

"I have an idea," said the sun. "You must go and live in the night and the darkness. At least that way they will not be able to see you weeping. And in time perhaps they will forget about you."

"You are right," said Amuwapi. "That is what I will do."

So Amuwapi went to live alone in the Palace of the Moon, where his children and their children and their children's children would never be able to see him weeping, and he left the whole wide world and all the thousand things for ever. And now his tears spread through the heavens to make the stars. Some of them stuck to the bodies of the frog Bes and the other creatures that had jumped into heaven to escape; but most of them ran together to make the great river of stars that flows in the sky. And that is a river they say will flow forever.

Bes, guardian demon of unknown origin, worshipped in Egypt; drawing after a relief in the Temple of Hatshepsut. According to tradition, frogs were sacrificed to him for protection from the evil eye and snakebite.

When the catfish had finished, there was a long slow silence.

"Tell me," said the wizard eventually. "Why are there no catfish in your story?"

"What is a catfish?" said the catfish.

"Oh, I suppose it doesn't really matter. But anyway, I must thank you for your story. You have kept your side of the bargain admirably, I would say. Better than you can understand. Perhaps you are not as stupid as you look."

"Why thank you," said the catfish.

"I only fear that your own reward will be less than satisfying. But anyway, you will find the peacock over there. He always comes to drink from that particular pool, just about now. Just follow that ridiculous screeching noise he makes and you will be sure to find him. And now I really should be running along myself, I suppose. I don't expect we'll be seeing each other again, so thanks once more, bon voyage and everything, and now you really must excuse me."

And suddenly he was gone.

Well, the catfish was very excited now. After all, he had come all the way to Persia for this moment! And even if he was a little tired after the long story, still he swam energetically enough down to the pool that the wizard had indicated. He swam round and round in his excitement; and sure enough, in a few minutes he heard the familiar screeching cry again: and there, stepping out from the trees, was the peacock himself at last!

Actually, the catfish couldn't help feeling a bit disappointed at his first sight of the creature he had come all the way to Persia to talk to. The peacock looked a bit like a chicken, he couldn't help thinking. But then he saw that the peacock was really rather a nice blue colour, and he did have some nice iridescent feathers, and he did have some bobbly bits on the top of his head . . . so maybe he was something special after all. Even if, as the owl had said all that long time ago, he did have a long and ridiculous tail, which dragged along so stupidly on the ground behind him.

"Hello," said the catfish. The peacock froze.

"Who said that?" it said suspiciously.

"Me," said the catfish, waving a fin out of the water.

"Oh..." said the peacock slowly, looking at the catfish with a growing expression of disgust. "I didn't know that anything as horrible as you existed. Ugh." He considered the catfish some more, as he swam round and round in the crystal clear water. "But really... you are just too revolting. Go away or I shall be ill." And the peacock looked pointedly in the opposite direction while he bent gracefully to the water to take a drink.

"Oh please, kind sir," said the catfish, with a note of desperation in his voice. "I have come a long way to see you today. It's terribly important." The peacock hesitated.

"Important?" he said dubiously. "Well, I suppose I can spare you a minute or two if it's really important. What's it about?"

"Love," said the catfish simply. The word had an electric effect on the peacock. He shivered convulsively from head to toe just at the sound of it.

"Love," he repeated slowly, as if the word itself was delicious in his mouth; and the catfish knew that he had come to the right place after all. The peacock strutted around a little, as if it was difficult to control his emotions, but in the end he managed to calm himself down long enough to continue. "Well, I suppose I do know something about *Love*," he conceded: and the word set him off again into a fresh flurry of sensuous shivering. "But what is it you want exactly?"

"I am searching for it," said the catfish; but to his horror and dismay, the peacock, after looking at him incredulously for a second, was overcome with screams of hysterical laughter.

"You?" it managed to gasp out eventually.

"Yes," said the catfish, trying to preserve his dignity. "I've been searching for it for some time, actually."

"I'm not surprised!" said the peacock, in between fresh screams of laughter. "Not surprised at all!" But the catfish just waited patiently, and in the end the peacock's laughter subsided to just a sort of quiet sarcastic giggle, which he could more or less control, it seemed. "So," he said. "Let's get this straight. You're searching for Love, and so you've come to me to see if I can give you some tips, eh? Is that more or less it?"

"More or less, I suppose," said the catfish miserably. It wasn't a laughing matter as far as he was concerned.

"Right," said the peacock. "Well. Let's see now." He tried to look serious about it, but as soon as he looked at the catfish again, just the thought of it was enough to set off a fresh round of giggling, and it took him some time to get himself back under control. "Sorry about that. Look, maybe it'll be easier if you just sort of ask me questions. How about that? I mean I'll do my best."

"Well . . . " The catfish tried to think about it. "Are there any sort of, I don't know, special tricks you could show me, maybe? That sort of thing?"

"Special tricks for finding love?" said the peacock, giggling.

"Yes," said the catfish seriously.

"Well. Hm. Yes. Let's see now." The peacock did his best to adopt a serious tone himself. "I don't really know where to start . . . I know! Tell me: are you familiar with the concept of fishing at all?" The catfish just looked at him. "Sorry. Oh yes. Of course you are. Well, all I'm trying to say, you see, is that what you have to use is some kind of *bait*."

"Bait?" said the catfish in an interested voice. This was more the sort of thing, he thought to himself.

"Yes. Exactly. Bait." The peacock nodded his head encouragingly, and all the bobbly bits bobbled about exotically. "Otherwise you get nowhere."

"Really," said the catfish. "How interesting. Maybe that's my problem . . . " But this only produced another fit of hysterical screeching from the peacock.

"Yes," he said. "Probably!"

"Well . . . " said the catfish, carefully, "You couldn't be a bit more sort of specific, could you?"

"Well, I don't want to discourage you, you know."

"No. But still . . . "

"Well, all right then. All right. But don't say I didn't warn you."

"I won't."

"Promise?"

"Promise."

"Well. This is the basic, er . . . "

"Bait?"

"Exactly." And with his practiced seducer's flourish, *whoosh*! he spread his fan in the sunshine and posed himself exquisitely against it. "There," he said, in a swaggering sort of voice.

"Ah."

"I did warn you."

"I know." But the catfish could hardly speak with pain and disappointment. Well, if that was what you needed to do to find Love, then it was hardly surprising, was it, that . . . But it really didn't bear thinking about. The peacock swivelled about a bit from side to side to exhibit the general effect a bit more, but it was like rubbing salt into the wound for the poor catfish.

"Isn't there anything else?" said the catfish after a while, more to take his mind off things than anything else. "Anything else I could try, I mean."

"Oh. Well, there is another sort of trick, actually. This is just the warm-up, actually. But I mean I don't want to depress you."

"Oh, don't worry about that," said the catfish stoically.

"All right then," said the peacock, who never needed much encouragement when it came to showing off. "This is what really does it." And he shook his tail so that it quivered like a tree in the wind, and all his hundred eyes rippled ecstatically around him, with a delicious quiet rustling sound. "Works every time," he confided. But suddenly he felt that he was wasting his talents – and anyway, he didn't really want to hurt the poor catfish's feelings. He couldn't help it if he looked like a slug with fins, now could he? He folded his tail up again and let it droop back down to the ground behind him. The catfish, though, had an idea.

"Like this?" he said, in a small voice; and the peacock looked on incredulously as the catfish, with huge concentration, thrashed his big fat grey old tail around from side to side behind him. It dislodged some mud from the bottom of the pool, and the mud rose in a nasty grey cloud around him as he concentrated on what he was doing. The peacock felt the screams of laughter coming again; but he managed to blurt out an unconvincing "Yes! Yes! That's it! You've got it!" before the effort became too much, and he fled helplessly off into the trees, convulsed again with screams of raucous laughter.

The catfish felt confused. This wasn't what he had been expecting at all. But still ... Perhaps he had learned something. Bait. Hmm. He thumped his tail around again, experimentally, although actually it didn't make much sense to him ... And suddenly there was a sort of flash, and the catfish found himself back on the outside of the gold and silver walls, back in the muddy water of the ditch where he had first met I Make No Promises, but with nowhere to go this time but home. Wherever that was. The owl and the wizard had been quite right, he thought irritably. That peacock really was a very foolish creature. And he began to wonder wearily which way he should travel next.

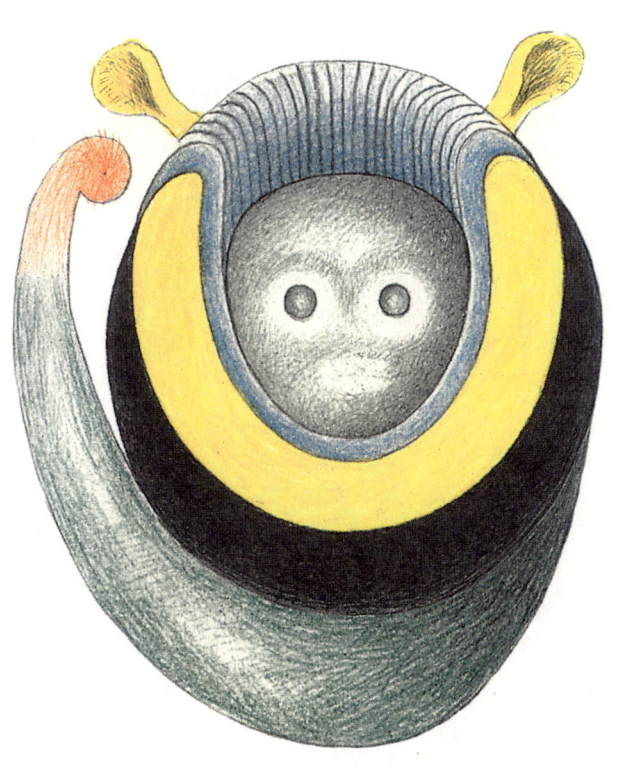

The man in rags had allowed himself to get quite carried away with his story. After all, it wasn't every day he got to perform for a Sultan, was it? But when he had finished, he realized with a shock that the Sultan, whom he had assumed to be just as caught up in it as he was himself, was actually fast asleep on his big soft sofa, and even – yes! – snoring slightly. It really was too bad. Still . . . the bottle, he realized, was not quite empty after all; and he was feeling quite a lot better on the whole, he thought . . . when suddenly, the Keeper of the Sultan's Treasure and the Keeper of the Sultan's Women and the Keeper of the Sultan's Hawks and Hounds all came rushing in together.

"Sh!" they all said to each other, holding their fingers to their lips, when they saw that the Sultan was sleeping. They all glared disapprovingly at the empty bottles, and then they all glared accusingly at the man in rags, who realized that his moment of glory was coming to an end.

"You wretch!" said one.

"You evil man!" said another.

"You criminal!" said the third, and the Keeper of the Sultan's Vultures and Crocodiles slipped a bottle into his pocket while he still had the chance.

"He's poisoned his Sublime Majesty!" said one.

"Led him astray!" said another.

"Oh dear!" said the third; and they all shook their heads very gravely. Then, suddenly, they all jumped on the man in rags, and soon they had him safely chained up again. You could never be too careful with the criminal element.

"What should we do with him now?" said one.

"To the crocodiles!" said another.

"No," said the third. They looked at him. "We can't."

"Can't?"

"Can't. What if the Sultan wants to see him again?"

"Eh?"

"What if the Sultan wants to see him again? What about that?"

"Yes! Yes! What if the Sultan wants to see me again?" said the man in rags enthusiastically. "What about that?"

"Watch it, you. Hm. I hadn't thought of that."

"Neither had I. Hm." And all three of them looked at their captive. They went off into a corner for an animated whispered conversation, and eventually the Keeper of the Hounds and Hawks announced the results of their deliberations.

"Very well. Seeing as how we admit that there might just be a possibility that his Sublime Majesty the Sultan might one day be so deluded as to require your presence again, and did not, contrary to our expectations, just have you thrown to the crocodiles as we would have liked, we have decided on this occasion to be generous."

"Magnanimous."

"Gracious."

"Exactly. Which is more than you deserve in my opinion." And they all nodded vigorously at that. "So, seeing as how you have managed to lead the Sultan into the debauch whose sad results are here before our eyes, and seeing as how we cannot entirely exclude the possibility that he will want to repeat the experience when he wakes up . . . "

"And seeing as how you don't want him to find out that there's no such position as Keeper of the Imperial Crocodiles and Vultures . . . " added the man in rags, maliciously.

"Sh! Sh!" they all said urgently. But the Sultan was still snoring away.

"For a variety of reasons," went on the Keeper of the Treasure, "It seems that we have little choice but to be lenient with you."

"Glad to hear it," said the man. "So it's back to the dungeons, is it?"

"Exactly. Let's go." And they all filed out, leading the man in rags away from his taste of luxury. The clanking of his chains disturbed some dream or other the Sultan was having, and he grumbled a bit in his sleep and shifted his weight a little on the sofa. And no-one noticed it, but the Sultan was smiling to himself with an expression of perfect contentment.

ΕΓΩ Η ΣΚΙΑΣ ΚΑΙ ΣΚΙΑΣ ΕΙΜΙ
ΚΑΙ ΤΟ ΑΙΜΑ ΜΟΥ ΕΣΤΙ
ΜΟΝΟΝ ΔΑΚΡΥ

Inscription found on the pedestal of a broken
mechanical statue, said to have been that of a weeping god.
Alexandria, c. 225 A.D.*

**Muinaisbysanttilainen jalustankaiverrus Aleksandriastä*, in "30 години финско-българска изледования", редакция К. Дж. О'Тул, Ангелина Инсарова, Институт на надписи на пиедестали, Българска академия на науките / Bysanttilainen-illyrialainen osasto, Jyväskylän yliopisto (1974), pp. 78-79.

FROM THE CATALOGUE OF MONSTROUS BIRTHS

In the province of Two Rivers, in the seventh moon, on the fifteenth day, in the fourth year of my office. *Be it recorded.* A male child was born to a woman of thirteen years. The child was in form like a frog, shorter than the usual length, but with long arms and legs, and webbed fingers and toes. There was no head, but eyes, nose and mouth were formed in the space between the shoulders. The skin was grey and smooth, cold, but without markings. The child was stillborn. The mother was examined and questioned in my presence, but denied any witchcraft or unnatural sexual congress. She was punished for ten days, and given for death by breaking. The child was burned and destroyed in my presence.
Great is Amuwapi, whose tears feed the day and the night.
My name is Gul-uhtru, and here is my seal.

Commentary In the constellation called the Frog, it is said that a watery mist has sometimes been observed at the time when great numbers of frogs appear in the mud of the Two Rivers. This is said to take place especially in the fourth moon, but also at other times. The constellation called the Frog is composed of seventeen stars; and it is recorded also that the frog Bes leaped into heaven at the beginning of the world, so that he would not have to swim for his life in the tears of Amuwapi below. The frog Bes teaches us wastefulness and ambition; but he also teaches us escape and success. *We order* that the fifteenth day of the seventh moon be remembered as the Day of the Punishment of Bes. It will be marked with the death by breaking of a woman of thirteen years, but without children.
Great is Amuwapi, who suffers as we do.
My name is Hivri, and here is my seal.

WHAT THE MERCHANT'S DAUGHTER THINKS ABOUT IT

We come across her as a lonely girl of fourteen lonely summers. That's how it seems to her, you understand. She weeps for love, in a general sort of way, she weeps for her loneliness, of course, and in particular she weeps in frustration and resentment at the harsh and unreasonable treatment she has received (and continues to receive!) from her father, a rich merchant who does not, she realizes, consider himself to be cruel – but then he does not consider himself to be rich either. His chief goal in life is to attain that blissful condition, certainly, but for some reason the closer he gets to it, the more easily it somehow manages to slip away at the last second. It recedes into the distance in front of him. He is not a happy man, anyway; but I'm sure that will not surprise you. It is a philosophical question, indeed, which of the two is the unhappier: the grasping capitalist or his tormented daughter. There are some other characters, incidentally, to be considered, but only really incidentally. We will enumerate them, just so we know where we are, but after that we will leave them to their own devices. Let's see. First of all there is the poor girl's mother: the merchant's wife, that is, and Mrs Bassari as we would say today. She is an exhausted and long-suffering sort, in her way, but in another way, and according to most people's standards (as if that ever counted for anything!), she is not long-suffering at all, for she passes her days and nights in the softest luxury. Furs and jewels have more or less silenced her, although most of the time she does still have enough of her wits about her to remember to keep up the steady stream of nagging demands for more. And actually the one single thing (though there are many) of all the many difficult things about her daughter that she will just positively never understand is her steady and thoughtless refusal to adopt the same general plan and attitude to life. It's not that the girl isn't greedy, you understand; she's greedy enough for two or three ordinary girls, that's for sure. No. She's got other things on her mind, that's her problem, and therein lies the seed of her failure to communicate with her dear old Ma, who, it seems, has never had anything much but the acquisition of material goods on hers. But we will come to that in a minute. Who's next? Ah yes. The real apple of the Bassari eye, the son and heir, young Abdul, but as he's still only seven he will remain something of a cipher for us. A personality too distant for scrutiny. Then there's a cook; a maid; and a gardener, porter and general handyman, also (by a coincidence) called Abdul. He combines these functions, you understand; and to tie the knot a little tighter, you should know that he's married to the cook and perpetually (though not so far successfully) trying to be unfaithful with the maid – a slovenly, fat girl, actually, but still she's twenty-four and he's fifty so what do you expect? Any other dramatis personae will be introduced as we go along, anyway, so let's get back to the moping teenager. She's shut herself up in her bedroom, of course, as teenage girls always have done and probably will do in perpetuity. And what exactly does she have her heart set on? A horse? Well, not exactly. The horse episode is a full year and a half ago already, and she'd rather not be reminded of it, anyway, because the burning but really quite *pure* desires (to call a spade a spade) that she used to feel towards horses in general and towards her own darling thoroughbred in particular suddenly and inexplicably evaporated when her thoughts (Oh shameful secret!) turned to men. Men! She could hardly even think of one without blinking and staring and going all funny as she put it to herself. There was also the important detail that she could hardly focus the resentment she now felt against her father (and which she urgently wanted to focus) by thinking about horses. He had been more than happy to indulge his baby girl, relying as usual on the secure-seeming hypothesis that he would be able to keep the female part of his household running smoothly along its emotional rail by means of nothing more difficult or demanding than regular bouts of expenditure. After all, it was the system he had always employed with the girl's mother, wasn't it? And so she had had stables and bridles and saddles and whatnot to her heart's content. He had soon noticed, in fact, that the proportion of actual riding involved in all this complicated business was always really rather small, even at the most intense and engulfing phase of her infatuation; but even from that small beginning he had been neither surprised nor (really) even particularly interested to see the proportion of riding to non-riding quickly diminish – almost, indeed, to zero. Still, he has written off the expenditure anyway (as if it was something for his wife) and so he hasn't lost any sleep over it. For that matter, it really wasn't quite in the very best of taste for the girl to go about on horseback. It marked her out immediately as one of the upper classes, but of course it wasn't as if there was really any problem about that. I mean it wasn't a problem with any real content to it, despite Bassari's endless agonizing over his balance sheets. And jewels or furs or actually just the mere mention of his name would have been quite enough to inspire an adequate quantity of awe and respect and all that sort of thing. Of course now he wishes that some such simple and practical solution as buying a horse or two would present itself. For Daddy I Want A Horse may quite conclusively be met with Here You Are Then; but all this sighing and hostility has unmanned him completely, he has to admit. He is flummoxed, that's what he is. And his wife unfortunately can offer no practical suggestions. Now, if their firstborn (well, not counting the one given up for the sacrifice, that is) had been a boy, then of course it would all be quite a different sort of thing. And this is no merely hypothetical or theoretical comparison, for there in the background is little Abdul, pulling the legs off flies or whatever it is that little boys do to amuse themselves, and Bassari knows that one day – one day! – young Abdul will be assailed by the emotional and, well, physical forces of adolescence too, and, why, then it will be no more than his fatherly duty to escort the little lad in person to the houses of pleasure where he is himself such a well-known and much-loved figure. "Much-loved" should be taken with a pinch of salt, of course. More of a commercial than an emotional assessment really. But then Bassari himself is more commercial than emotional, isn't he, and proud of it too, you know. He has never allowed his emotions to get in the way of his business. Such a thing would simply never have occurred to him. And so it is doubly or trebly galling to be confronted with the fact that the normal healthy equilibrium of his household is being not simply threatened, but actually positively disturbed by the unsteady flux of his daughter's emotions. And he has done his best, hasn't he? Of course he has. There is that beautiful necklace in lapis lazuli and mother of pearl, isn't there? And that would have been more than enough to earn him a few day's peace and harmony in the good old days, before the ridiculous girl discovered (as he supposed she had) love and its complications. A nice new bracelet for Daddy's Girl. It is the same system he has always used with females – family members, clients' wives, *filles de joie* – and it has never failed him yet. Until now, that is. Well, it is perplexing for him. Worse than that: it threatens to unbalance his business judgement, as he tells himself in a shocked internal voice. And so at last something will have to be done. But actually, the thing is, what is really unbalancing him is not so much the worry as the fact that his daughter's mooning about has taken on a decidedly erotic aspect; and yes, that is something he does find very unbalancing after all this time. She is, he can see, preparing herself for love, and of course it is all entirely natural and instinctive and all the rest of it, but still . . . he has no means of defending himself against the erotic appeal of her presence and her behaviour, however certainly he knows as a parent that he must deny and defeat this temptation. For after all, under different circumstances a teenage girl who chose to spend the whole day wandering around in her pyjamas would arouse a different and well-rehearsed set of responses in him. But when it is his own daughter who appears like that, half-dressed and apparently still half-asleep, to pick absent-mindedly at some grapes or some marzipan or whatever it is, he knows that his duty lies elsewhere than in the appreciation of her languid curves and graceful limbs. Her hips and her eyes swivel about: but not for him. And he tries to take a firm line, if only because the girl's mother is putting pressure on him. The girl needs a husband, that's the main thing. A husband. But all she has to do is knit her brows in that one particular way and all his resolve just vanishes. And the girl herself? What secret passions make her shapely young breast flutter like that? Does she dream of a solid young businessman and a life of luxury and acquisition? Ah no. For she wants, you see, someone special. It is only natural. For there are any number of pampered young men . . . Well, actually, she is wrong about that. The reason she is experiencing all this crisis in the first place is simply that the boy her father has picked out for her future bridegroom is himself, like Abdul, only seven years old. Everything is so *difficult*! If only, if only ... If only he had produced his son and daughter the other way around! For if the son were fourteen and the daughter were seven, then everything else in the world would surely be perfect too. For his ... well, no, not really his *friend* exactly, that would be going a little bit too far, but what shall we say his esteemed and valued business partner shall we say has now more or less agreed to the union of their fortunes, and marriage is obviously the best way to manage it. The problem has arisen, though, that when he tried to introduce the future bridegroom into the household, the wrong kind of result entirely was produced. For his own son, namely young Abdul had pounced joyfully on the boy for a playmate, while the stupid girl (that's how he thinks of her) had barely even noticed him. And while the boys are playing at camels or whatever it is they play at on the floor, he can hardly be expected to raise the topic of matrimony, now can he? But anyway the poor girl (or the rich girl, really, if the truth be told) has quite another sort of project in mind than the distasteful commercial venture planned by her scheming father. For deep down in her soft secret self she longs only for the deep brown eyes of the madman and poet she sees sometimes in the market square, and who seems to have so scandalized the town with his immoderate behaviour and declarations. And that's that. She sighs. And he has probably never even noticed her. It is all enough to make a girl really quite cross. Not to mention frustrated. Round her feet her future husband crawls and shouts, lost in some boys-will-be-boys kind of fantasy world; and all that she can do is to sigh miserably. Sigh. And she pulls in absent-minded irritation at the sleeve of her silk pyjamas with a filed and polished nail. Oh, but has he noticed her really? Has he?

Cartouche and inscription allegedly from the tomb (or temple?) of Ammu-Wab, legendary (and perhaps fictitious) God-Pharaoh of the Second Dynasty (3rd millennium B.C.). Drawing made by an unknown correspondent of Prof. Klipsten. No-one has been able to identify the site or location from which the drawing is supposed to have come. Hannig's authoritative *Großes Handwörterbuch Ägyptisch-Deutsch* includes a record of the inscription in this cartouche (pg. 1257), but with an extraordinary triple disclaimer, viz. *Ammu-Wab Vergöttlicher Pharao [?] Existenz des Gottes nicht gesichert; Existenz des Königs nicht gesichert; Existenz des Wortes nicht gesichert.*

SONG OF THE SLAVE GIRL

My master is the lord Ammu-Wab
I am the shadow of his shadow
He lives alone in the Moon
I am the shadow of his shadow
Until the end of the world
In the morning I attend to him
In the evening I attend to him
My lady Nut supports the heavens
Until the end of the world
My lord Osiris cares for the dead
Until the end of the world
I will attend to my lord Ammu-Wab
For I am the shadow of his shadow
Until the end of the world

Hieroglyphic inscription, Upper Egypt, 2nd Dynasty (c. 2500 BC). Found on the remains of the sarcophagus thought to have contained the mummified remains of a young girl, the victim of a human sacrifice. The sarcophagus had been broken by looters and the mummy removed. Next to the sarcophagus was found an earthenware jar containing a mummified fish.

KING MU'S JOURNEY TO HEAVEN*
穆天子天堂之行

From the Zhou Dynasty "Book of Dreams" (梦书), traditionally ascribed to the legendary Yu (禹), but assumed to be the work of many hands.

It is said that during his great journey around the world, the King of Mu came to a certain place where strange visions and other wonders were produced. Sending his retinue away, he lay down to sleep alone in that place, and fell into a sort of trance, during which time he had the dream recorded here.

• • •

It seemed to me that I was lifted from the earth, and that I sped through the air like an arrow from a bow, or like time itself, which reduces all our projects to nothing. And after a very long time, I saw the glow of heaven before me, and in my ears there was the glad music of that far-off land, and in a minute I came to rest among a crowd of graceful ladies, who laughed and danced and ate peaches and drank from silver cups. Everything was silk and luxury and happiness; but I perceived with a shock that I alone was dressed in the rags of the lowest beggar, and when I reached out my hand to touch the peaches of immortality (for that, I knew, was the food on which the ladies were feasting so carelessly), they drove me off with taunts and laughter. "We see by your rags that this is not the food for you!" they said, and instead they threw some cabbages on the ground at my feet. "If you are hungry, then eat!" they said, and they went back to their games and their dancing.

I sat down on a stone and began to weep, for now I knew that I would never taste those golden peaches or know what it was that lay in those sparkling silver

---

*From *A Classical Chinese Reader*, Vol. 1, (Beijing: Foreign Languages Press, 1976).

goblets. The crowd of ladies went on their way, it seemed, and when I was alone, and weeping quietly, as I have said, I was disturbed instead by a small golden dragon, who carried a silver spear. I guessed that he must be an official of some kind, and so I was not surprised when he told me to state my occupation and my business. I found that my answer was ready in my mouth, though I wondered myself at the words that came.

"I cannot remember what my name is," I told him, "But my occupation is that of a beggar and nothing more."

"And yet," said the dragon, "It would appear from your speech and your manner that you are a person of some learning and cultivation. I would advise you to resolve this paradox for me, since I, sir, am charged expressly with removing any beggars or highwaymen or other ruffians. We do not tolerate any such people in heaven, I'm afraid."

"You are right," I said. "As you observe, it is fate alone that has reduced me to this depressing condition. Once I rode with a fine retinue. My head was shaded with silken parasols, my feet were clothed in gold brocade, and my apartments rang with the disputations of the learned. And now . . . " But I could not contain my weeping.

"Come, come," said the dragon. "This will not do. You had better acquaint me with the details, or I shall be compelled to expel you!"

"Oh, very well," I sighed. "It is a commonplace enough story, after all. My father, you see, was a magistrate in the service of the Emperor. He held a number of degrees and was a man of some discernment when it came to matters of literary taste, legal expertise, and so on. The same, however, cannot be said for his judgement of human nature. His deficiencies in that regard became clear to all when, although already a man of mature years, he took it into his head to marry a young and beautiful wife. Filial duty naturally prevented any direct opposition to this scheme of his, but I will confess that by various sideways methods I did what I could to agitate against such a result; and the efforts of my relations tended mostly in the same direction. He was already married, after all, as we pointed out, and there were other, equally convincing, arguments, we thought. But he had fixed his mind upon the course of retrieving his youthful vigour by means of regular union with some junior accomplice; and marriage, it seemed to him, was the surest and most dignified means to effect such a plan. We assured him that for a man of his years and position to adopt such a view of things was assuredly nothing but the symptom of some sickness in his mind, and that a course of healthy exercise, and perhaps a change of diet, would be a much more prudent system. We counselled drugs and herbal infusions. More privately, we suggested that such experiments as he suggested could also (or instead!) be carried out in certain commercial establishments of more or less questionable reputation, but nevertheless certainly well-equipped for such therapies as he probably had in mind. But it was all to no avail, and soon my father introduced into our household a person who, while certainly falling into the age-group the fantasies of his condition had indicated as the most propitious for the type of regeneration he had in mind, apparently had nothing much else to recommend her.

"Had she employed some sinister necromancer or mercenary druggist to ensnare the white-haired patriarch? It was only natural that our suspicions should propel our thoughts in such a direction. But however she had managed it, once she was installed in the house, we knew that from then on we could no longer truly call it our own. My father's jade and porcelain was all packed up and labelled – catalogued, we knew, for eventual sale and distribution. The furniture, the books and manuscripts, why, even the chests and wardrobes of our clothes were rifled for anything remotely saleable. My father, though, grew steadily more distant from us, under the baleful influence of the vixen. She raised the spectre of financial catastrophe before his eyes, and told him, we knew, that it was we who were to blame, with our expensive and unproductive ways. She placed documents in his shaking hands, and he signed and sealed them with his failing forces. Little by little, we were stripped of all our possessions, until at last the old man came to the end of everything. He was convinced to his last breath that he was in the grip of a miraculous transformation; but we knew that his death had been hastened by the avarice of the stranger in our midst. He died with her cynical laughter ringing in his ears."

"Yes," said the dragon, a little peevishly, I thought. "It is certainly a commonplace enough story. You are reduced, I suppose, to desperate poverty, and forced to beg by the roadside?"

"That is more or less it."

"There are many such as you. The vixen, I suppose, has moved on, in search of fresh victims?"

"She has."

"Well, I'm afraid that if that is really the whole situation then I will simply have to ask you to move on. We can't allow the place to get cluttered up with people such as you." He lifted his silver spear in a hostile and efficient manner. "Or is there something else you can add?"

"There is one small thing," I said, pulling out a folded paper. "My father, as I told you, was a man of some discernment in literary matters, and, once, when he was approaching the end, he gave me this strange little story. It is all that I have to mark my case out as unusual."

"And what is it called?" said the dragon, hesitantly.

"It is called *The Catfish and the Slave-girl*. Shall I read it out loud to you?"

"Please," said the dragon.

THE CATFISH AND THE SLAVE-GIRL

There was once a slave-girl who knew everything in the world except how to be happy. She could cook and clean and sew and make carpets and blankets and eiderdowns, but for some reason whatever she did she just could not find any contentment in it. And that meant that no-one else found any pleasure in being with her, and so it was all very sad. She worked and worked from morning to night, and never complained or got angry or caused any trouble; the thing was, no-one ever really noticed her, or wondered if she was happy, and she thought that she would just have to spend the rest of her life cooking and cleaning and sewing and making carpets and blankets and eiderdowns. But no-one even noticed that she was unhappy.

Now, one day the cook called her into the kitchen and said, "I have something for you to do. We have caught a strange-looking fish in the river, but we don't know what to do with it. We don't know if it is good to eat, or how it should be cooked, or anything about it at all. Since you are so clever, we thought that perhaps you might be able to tell us. It is outside in a bucket in the garden."

The slave-girl stopped what she was doing and went out to look at the strange fish. It swam around and around in the bottom of its bucket and looked up at her. "It's a catfish," she thought to herself. "I wonder how it got here?" And she started thinking about how she could cook it. With onions, perhaps? Or just grilled with some lemon . . . But suddenly the catfish spoke to her, and she was very surprised.

"I hope you are not planning to eat me," said the catfish.

"That's what we normally do with fish that we catch," said the slave-girl.

"Oh, but in my case I really think you should make an exception."

"Well that does not surprise me. Tell me, what are you doing here?"

"I am searching for Love."

"Love?"

"Love." And the catfish flicked his tail from side to side, a bit half-heartedly. "I have been searching for it for a long time now. I don't suppose you know where

I might find it?"

"Not really," said the slave-girl. "Have you lost it?"

"Oh no. I have never had it. I don't even know what it looks like. But I have been all the way to Persia to look for it."

"Well if we eat you then at least that will put an end to it," said the slave-girl. And she picked the bucket up to take it into the kitchen. After all, there was work to be done.

"Wait!" said the catfish. "Perhaps we can come to some sort of understanding! I have been travelling for many years, and so I know all sorts of useful things. If you let me go, perhaps there is some secret I could tell you in return!"

"Oh, nonsense," said the slave-girl crossly. "I already know everything there is to know. For instance, I know that you will be very nice grilled with some lemon."

"Oh no!" said the catfish miserably. "So now I will never find Love."

"Well I can't do anything about that," said the slave-girl. But the catfish looked so miserable that something snapped inside her. She just couldn't do it. She put the bucket down again. "Look," she said. "I don't know why I should do this, but I suppose I could tell them that you're very poisonous and bad luck too, and that we should throw you back immediately."

"Yes! Yes!" said the catfish. "Good idea!"

"But what will you do if I let you go?"

"Oh, I will keep on searching! And I'm sure that if you let me go, then I will be sure to succeed in the end."

"Really?"

"Really! I'm quite sure of it."

"Well . . . " She looked at the catfish and thought about it. "All right then." And the catfish flicked his tail from side to side for joy. The slave-girl went into the kitchen, and in a minute she was back. "It's all right. I told them that you are a poison-fish from Persia, and very bad luck, and that we should throw you back immediately."

"Oh, thank you!" said the catfish happily. And he sounded so pleased that the slave-girl couldn't help smiling a little to herself. She picked up the bucket and took it down to the river – and with one quick movement the catfish found himself wriggling through the air and *splash*! back into the water where he belonged. He waved a fin out of the water to the slave-girl.

"Thank you!" said the catfish.

"Goodbye!" said the slave-girl. "And good luck!"

And the catfish swam off alone to carry on searching for Love.

"Well!" said the dragon when I had finished. "That *is* a strange story. What does it all mean?"

"I'm afraid I don't really know," I said. But it is the only thing I possess apart from these rags you see me wearing. I realize it's not much."

"Hmm..." said the dragon, thoughtfully. "Perhaps there is one thing we could try. For it is always a reprehensible duty to have to expel a gentleman, you know."

"Oh, I can appreciate that. What do you have in mind?"

"Not far from here, there is a place they call the Palace of the Moon, and in that Palace there lives a strange old god. Amu Wabi is his name. He devotes himself, like you, to endless lamentation and dreary weeping."

"And is he a being of some discernment, then?"

"Your mind is one of rare penetration. I know that in the past he has expressed an interest in curious tales and stories. Perhaps this one of yours will be to his taste."

"There is no harm in trying it."

"You are right. I will take your paper to him immediately, if you permit it, and we will see what he has to say."

"Very well." And I gave up the paper to the golden dragon, who disappeared with it. I returned to my weeping, of course, and in a while the dragon was back.

"You're in luck," he said.

"Really?"

"I think so. I showed your story to Amu Wabi, and he said he was very pleased with it. Showed rare literary discernment and good taste, he said."

"I told you that my father was a man of some talent."

"That's as may be. Anyway, he has given me some instructions. We have discussed the matter of your expulsion, and we have managed to come to a compromise. He says that he fully sympathises with your decision to devote yourself to weeping and lamentation, and in the normal course of events he would simply grant you your heart's desire to put a stop to it. However..."

"What?"

"Well, could I ask you what your heart's desire is, exactly?"

"Oh. Well . . . I think I should like to taste the peaches of immortality, and join that happy throng of beautiful women who were here just now. Come to think of it."

"Yes. We were afraid of that. For now you have seen them, we know that you will never be satisfied with that weary mortal life below."

"I suppose not."

"Very well then. This is what we will do. I am afraid that we will have to expel you now, for your thoughts are full of the stains and the dirt of the world, and so we cannot allow you to come among us. But now that you have been here for a little while, you will appear as one of us to those below; and great wealth and magical powers will be yours. But you will be all alone, with no-one to call a friend. If you weep for long enough, then in time you will have wept out all the pain and ugliness of the world. But you must live alone, and resist the temptation to use your magical powers to enslave others. And then, one day, when you have wept out all your suffering in the world, and when you have lived all alone for long enough to have forgotten the man you once were, then you may come back among us and taste the peaches of immortality." I thought about this and tried to understand it.

"It will be a weary time," I said. "But I will do it. I will go to Persia, I think, and live alone. But tell me, how will I know when the time has come for me to return?"

"You will know," said the dragon. "Oh yes, and there is one other thing. Amu Wabi said that your father's story lacked an ending. He has provided one. He suggests you take it and contemplate it at your leisure." And he returned the piece of paper to me. I unfolded it, and saw that a few lines of writing had been added at the bottom, in characters of immortal perfection.

The slave-girl had never known what it was to perform an act of generosity. She never learned whether the catfish found Love in the end, but little by little a great change came over her. She began to perform small kindnesses for others, and to ask for no reward; and soon she learned to smile and even to laugh a little sometimes. And one day a young man came to make her heart glad.

And that is how my dream ended.

THE PHOENIX*

In Yunnan there is told a children's story concerning the phoenix and Amu Wabi. No-one can tell where it came from, or what it means.

The phoenix was not always immortal, you know. Once upon a time it was just an ordinary bird. But it looked at all the other birds and thought: I will be better than all of them. I will fly higher than the eagle, I will be more beautiful than the peacock, and I will be wiser than the owl. For I am the phoenix, and there is only one of me.

So the phoenix asked the Man in the Moon (whose name was Amu Wabi) how he could be wiser than the owl, and how he could be more beautiful than the peacock, and how he could fly higher than the eagle; and this was his answer. "You will never fly higher than the eagle, or be wiser than the owl, or be more beautiful than the peacock. But you are the phoenix, and there is only one of you."

The phoenix was so sad that he cried and cried and cried. So Amu Wabi burned him in a magic fire. But he could not burn his shadow, and so the shadow became immortal. And every little tongue of flame you see is nothing but a little piece of the shadow of the phoenix. For the phoenix will live forever, and there is only one of him.

Chinese character for Phoenix; calligraphy by Wang Suo-Cheng.

---

*Adapted from *Folk Tales Of South-West China*, ed. Wendy Wang, (Hong Kong: Phoenix Publishing Corp., 1987).

THE SULTAN AND THE MAN IN RAGS AGAIN

Well, when he woke up the Sultan had been a little surprised to find that the amusing if badly-dressed storyteller was no longer there. But the palace officials had explained to him that the man had been forced to go and attend to the vultures and the crocodiles, and the Sultan had accepted this explanation without too much trouble. He was suffering from some strange illness, anyway, feeling very sick and thirsty, and with the most appalling headache too. And what with one thing and another, he had quite forgotten about his loneliness.

A few days later, though, it was back, just as bad as before; and the Sultan felt just as miserable. Desperate, even.

"I know!" he said.

"What, sire?" said the officials.

"I need to be entertained, that's what."

"Very good, sire." And the Keeper of the Sultan's Women made to clap his hands; but the Sultan stopped him with an angry gesture.

"No, no. Not like that. Tell me, what about that splendid story-telling fellow who was here a few days ago? You know the one."

"Ah yes. The Doctor."

"Not the Doctor, you fool! Anyway, didn't we have him thrown to the crocodiles?"

"Not exactly, sire."

"The vultures, then."

"I'm afraid not."

"Pity. I must confess my memory is a little hazy for some reason. But anyway, I mean the other fellow that was here. You know. The one in the amusing costume." But the officials all did their best to look puzzled. "I remember!" said the Sultan, slapping his knee. "The Keeper of the Vultures and Crocodiles!"

"Oh."

"Oh yes."

"Him."

"Yes. Him. A most diverting fellow! Send for him, would you?"

"But . . ."

"Yes?"

"Well . . ."

"What is it?"

"Oh, very well. It's just that . . . Well, we're not sure that he's really the right sort of person for Your Sublime Majesty to be consorting with, that's all."

"Who is the Sultan around here, may I ask?"

"Yes, sire."

"Well send for him, then!"

"At once, sire."

"That's better. Really!"

And the Sultan settled himself on his cushions expectantly. After a few minutes, the same man in rags was hustled back into the royal presence. He shook off the friendly hands that gripped his upper arms, and bowed gravely.

"Majesty," he said, rubbing at his wrists in a curious manner.

"My dear fellow! How are you? But come, come, sit yourself down and entertain me. That's it. Relax. How are the crocodiles?"

"Oh. Yes. Very happy." The man seemed to hesitate, but then he seemed to relax and let himself go a little. "Yes. They had an Armenian today, actually. Well, most of an Armenian. There were a few bits missing by the time they got their teeth into him, though, Your Majesty. Just between you and me." And he winked hideously.

"How do you mean exactly?" said the Sultan, enthralled.

"People take bits for charms, you see."

"No!"

But the man in rags nodded seriously, "Oh yes. Body parts."

"What people? And what parts?"

"Oh, I'm sorry. I didn't mean to shock you. It's the guards, mainly. They do it on commission."

"But . . . But that's dreadful! Do you really mean to tell me that there's a trade in body parts? *Bits*, as you put it? It's horrible!"

"Horrible is about right. But that's not the half of it. Not the half of it, I say! Oh, I could tell you some stories . . . "

"I'm sure you could. But look, I don't really think we need to go into all this now. Tell me . . . "

"Yes?"

"You haven't got anything to drink, have you?"

"Ah!" The man in rags smiled and winked expressively. "I had a feeling you might ask me that." He produced a bottle. "Armenian. Oh, don't look at me like that. It's one of the few privileges of my profession."

And half an hour later they were the best of friends again. The Sultan smiled benignly, and the man in rags was at his most entertaining, it seemed, chattering on about this and that in a most unusual manner. If only everyone in the palace was as amusing as this, the Sultan thought.

"If only everyone in the palace was as amusing as you!" he said affably.

"Oh, but then you wouldn't notice the difference any more," said the man. "It would just mean a lot more effort all around, and you'd be just as bored with it all in the end. But tell me, how's the loneliness?"

"Oh." The Sultan let out a great sigh.

"Just the same, eh?"

"Worse."

"Well, I'm sorry to hear that. I don't really know what to suggest."

"Oh, it's not your fault. But do tell me . . . "

"Yes?"

"I did so enjoy your story last time, you know. I mean I realize I fell asleep, but it was awfully long."

"Hm," said the man in rags.

"And I only missed a little bit. Just the very end of it."

"Just the end," repeated the man in rags dismally.

"Yes, I know. I really am terribly sorry. But I promise I'll try to stay awake this time. Really. Perhaps you could try a slightly shorter one."

"Well . . . " The Sultan smiled at him encouragingly. "All right then."

And they filled their glasses, as before.

AMUWAPI AND THE SLAVE-GIRL*

They say that Amuwapi once had a slave-girl, who looked after him in the Palace of the Moon. Where she came from I don't know, and what became of her in the end I couldn't tell you, but this is her story.

"Amuwapi!" she said one day, in a cross sort of voice. "I really can't understand why it is that you sit there day after day crying like that. Look at me! I work from morning until night, cleaning and cooking and making blankets and curtains and eiderdowns and whatnot, and you don't see me sitting around all day crying about it, do you?"

"You don't understand," said Amuwapi.

"Well I don't know about that; but isn't there anything I could do to stop you from crying? Even just for one day? For otherwise I really think that I will lose my mind."

Amuwapi thought about this. He didn't want the slave-girl to lose her mind, after all.

"I tell you what," he said. "I will make an agreement with you. If you can make the sun stand still in the sky, then I will stop my weeping long enough to take a look at him. That is what I will do. But for now you must excuse me." And he went back to his tears and lamentation.

Well, the next day the slave-girl put her hat on, and she put her gloves on, and she put her coat on.

"You'll have to get your own lunch," she said to Amuwapi. "For now I am going off to see how I can make the sun stand still in the sky."

"Very well," said Amuwapi. And off she went. And after a time she came upon

---

*Adapted from "The girl from the river Zanga" in *Armenian Folk Stories*, R.J. Hamilton, ed., Ch. 4, New York, 1976. For ML.

a man in a red shirt. He was standing in her way, and she could not continue.

"You cannot continue along this road until you have answered my question," he said.

"But I am sent by Amuwapi to make the sun stand still in the sky!" she said.

"Well I don't know anything about that. All I know is that unless you answer my question, I will never let you past."

"In that case I will curse you forever," said the slave-girl. "But hurry up and tell me your question, for I am in great haste, and cannot stop here for you."

"Very well. What is it that shows and does not show; what is it that hides nothing and hides everything; what is it that turns beauty to ugliness and ugliness to beauty? That is my question to you." And he folded his arms expectantly.

"Oh, that's easy," said the slave-girl. "It is a mirror. In the light it shows and in the dark it does not show. It hides nothing that is in front of it and it hides everything that is behind it. In the hands of an unhappy woman it turns beauty to ugliness. In the hands of a vain woman it turns ugliness to beauty. Now let me pass."

"You may pass," said the man in the red shirt. "For that is the answer to my question." And the slave-girl continued on her way. But she gave her hat to the man as a toll.

After a time, she came upon a woman in a yellow dress. The woman was standing in the road, and the slave-girl could not continue.

"Do you have a question for me?" said the slave-girl.

"I have no question for you," said the woman. "For I come from the Underworld, and I know everything already."

"In that case," said the slave-girl, "I suppose you must know how I can make the sun stand still in the sky. For that is the only way for me to stop Amuwapi from weeping."

"Of course I know how to make the sun stand still in the sky. Nothing could be simpler. All I would need is a needle and a piece of chalk. But what could you offer me in return?"

"I know how to cook and clean, and I can make very good blankets and eiderdowns."

"I am not interested in such commonplace things. Will you give me your heart?" But the slave-girl would not give her heart to the woman in the yellow dress.

"Will you give me your head?" But the slave-girl would not give her head to the woman in the yellow dress.

"Will you give me your hands?" The slave-girl tried to trick the woman in the yellow dress by giving her her gloves, but the woman just laughed and spat on the ground.

"I will take your gloves as a present to my husband, who is the King of the Underworld. You must wait for me here until I return, and if you do not have a present for me when I come back, I will take your heart and your head and your hands anyway."

"In that case I will curse you forever," said the slave-girl. But the woman in the yellow dress went away to the Underworld, and the slave-girl had nothing to do but wait.

After a time, an old, old man came hobbling very slowly along the road. When he came closer, the slave-girl could see that he was following an ant that was crawling along the road in front of him. On his back he had a big leather bag. But the slave-girl stood in the road, so that they could go no further.

"What do you have in your bag?" she asked the old man.

"The wind," replied the man. "The West Wind and the South Wind and the East Wind and the North Wind. For I have caught them all and put them in this bag."

"Well now you can go no further," said the slave-girl, "for I must have a present for the Queen of the Underworld when she returns, and I think I will take your bag of wind."

"But what will you give me in return?" said the man.

"I will give you my coat and nothing else. And then you may continue on your way." And the slave-girl took the bag away from the man's shoulders and spread her coat there instead. And the man went on his way.

When the Queen of the Underworld returned, she asked the slave-girl what present she had found for her.

"I have the West Wind for you."

"But I do not want the West Wind."

"I have the South Wind for you."

"But I do not want the South Wind."

"I have the East Wind for you."

"But I do not want the East Wind."

"I have the North Wind for you."

"But I do not want the North Wind."

"Then I will curse you forever!" shouted the slave-girl, and she opened the old man's bag and threw it over the head of the Queen of the Underworld. The Queen of the Underworld turned into a mouse, but the slave-girl caught her in the bag. The Queen of the Underworld turned into a hare, but the slave-girl caught her in the bag. The Queen of the Underworld turned into fire and water, but the slave-girl caught her in the bag and held her forever. But the West Wind and the South Wind and the East Wind and the North Wind ran round and round, and round and round they ran, and in a minute they made the whirlwind, and the whirlwind lifted the slave-girl up into the sky to see the sun.

"If you will stand still in the sky for me," she said, "Then I will give you a bag of fire and water, and the Queen of the Underworld will be yours for a slave." And the slave-girl danced through the clouds on the back of the whirlwind, until she reached the Palace of the Moon.

"Look! Look!" she said. "The sun is standing still in the sky!" And Amuwapi stopped his weeping to look. And the slave-girl danced over the clouds and snatched her hat from the man in the red shirt, and she snatched her coat from the old, old man, and she even danced down into the world that cannot be seen and snatched her gloves back from the King of the Underworld, and then she came back laughing to the Palace of the Moon, and Amuwapi did not weep for all the time that the sun stood still in the sky.

But then the West Wind brought the thunder, and the North Wind brought the lightning, and the East Wind brought the storm, and the South Wind brought the flood, and the sun called out to Amuwapi, for he did not know what to do. But the Queen of the Underworld clapped her hands once, and the storm was tamed. She clapped her hands twice, and the flood was tamed. She clapped her hands three times, and the thunder was tamed. She clapped her hands four times, and the lightning was tamed. And she said to the sun, "I will never be your slave. For you do not know how to keep fire and water in a bag." And she ran away to her husband in the Land of the Dead.

The sun stood still no longer, and in a minute Amuwapi began to weep once more. The slave-girl took off her hat, and she took off her coat, and she took off her gloves. For now she knew that Amuwapi would weep forever.

The man in rags was not surprised to see that the Sultan had fallen asleep again. But he had continued his story to the end anyway, because he knew that the Keeper of the Women and the Keeper of the Money and the Keeper of the Hawks and Hounds were hiding around the corner and listening. He had managed to slip a jewelled paper-knife into his pocket when no-one was looking, which was something, but he wasn't surprised when they all rushed in and bound him with chains again. They all tried not to make the chains clank too loudly as they dragged him away, and the Sultan just carried on snoring quietly on his cushions. He was smiling a gentle smile, though: for in his dream, the slave-girl was dancing through the clouds.

TEXT FOR A RELIGIOUS RITUAL*

Priest   I stand in the light. In the light I stand.
I stand in the shadow. In the shadow I stand.
I will not speak my name. My name has no meaning.
I will not use my eyes. My eyes may deceive me.
I will repeat the words that are written in stone.
The words that are written in stone will not deceive me.

I begin the invocation. Now I begin the prayer.
I call to Amuwapi. I call to Amuwapi who weeps forever.
I remember his tears. His tears are in my eyes.
I remember his lamentation. His voice is in my mouth.
I will repeat the words that are written in stone.
The words that are written in stone will not deceive me.

Victim   I have come.

Priest   Who are you?

Victim   I do not know.

Priest   Who are you?

Victim   It does not matter.

Priest   Who are you?

Victim   I have forgotten.

---

*Mohenjo-Daro, Indus Valley glyphic inscription, c. 2250 BC.

Priest   Why are you here?

Victim   I am ready.

Priest   Why are you here?

Victim   I am ready.

Priest   Why are you here?

Victim   I am ready.

Priest   Say the words.

Victim   I am the shadow of a shadow of a shadow,
And my blood is nothing but a teardrop.

Priest   Will the fields be fruitful?

Victim   Yes.

Priest   Will the thousand things multiply forever?

Victim   Yes.

Priest   Say the words.

Victim   I am the shadow of a shadow of a shadow,
And my blood is nothing but a teardrop.

Priest   Will the rivers bring fish?

Victim   Yes.

Priest   Will the clouds bring rain?

Victim   Yes.

Priest   Will the sun continue in the sky?

Victim   Yes.

Priest   Say the words.

Victim   I am the shadow of a shadow of a shadow,
And my blood is nothing but a teardrop.

Priest   Now I take the knife. In my hand I hold the knife.
Amuwapi, speak with my tongue. Amuwapi, see with my eyes.
Amuwapi, hear with my ears. Amuwapi, feel with my heart.
Here is the blood that flows. Here are your tears that flow.
Here is the heart that beats. Here is the heart that suffers.
Here is the head for the fire. Here is the head we will burn.
Here are the hands for the earth. Here are the hands we will bury.

I have repeated the words that are written in stone.
The words that are written in stone have not deceived me.

When we broke at last into the burial chamber, we were cruelly disappointed to find that thieves had come there before us once again. There was nothing that was not smashed or ruined, and it was clear that much had been removed — though how much, or how long ago, we could not tell. Not a bead, not a jewel or a piece of wire had been left. Indeed, it seemed that the thieves still mocked us, for they had scratched and defaced the inscription that stood on the far wall so thoroughly that it is useless to think that we will ever be able to read it. Where they had broken through the wall above the inscription, presumably to effect their entry (since the sealed door through which we entered had not been opened or disturbed), there were the remains of a frieze; and some fragments of this were eventually found in the rubbish on the floor of the chamber. The frieze seems to have represented a procession and sacrifice of serving-women, and we have speculated that the upper, broken, part of the frieze may have contained a representation of the royal funeral itself. To add to our unhappiness, a cache of unmarked earthenware jars that we found in the southeastern corner of the chamber, buried under a layer of sand and rubble, turned out to contain nothing but thirty-four pairs of human hands, severed at the wrists. We examined these carefully, but found no rings, bracelets, or other jewelry. Neither did we find any inscriptions, or anything else.

>Sir Hugo Smyth, *Excavations in Mesopotamia,* London, 1923

Among the Xan (or Zan) people of the central massif there is told a tale of a great Khan in the sky, who holds the fate of all the tribes in his hands. He is said to weep constantly, and the stars are said to be his tears.

Among the women there is preserved a version of the story told as a sort of game. Girls take it in turns to ask questions in rhyme concerning the house of this Khan, to which they receive cryptic answers from the older women, who also correct any mistakes made in the formulation of the questions.

Captain Reynolds reports the following exchange as typical:

> Why should I go when it is so far, so far?
> For I would be so tired, so tired.

> *You should go there for love*
> *But you will not find it*
> *Until the sun stands still in the sky!*

> And how should I get there all alone, all alone?
> For surely my shadow will catch me.

> *You must go there for love*
> *By the light of the moon*
> *Run away while your shadow is sleeping!*

Bradley, *Compendium of Ethnography*, Chicago, 1928

THE SULTAN AND THE MAN IN RAGS ONCE MORE

"I say, you haven't seen a rather nice gold paper-knife, decorated with garnets and sapphires, have you?" said the Sultan, the next time he saw his friend.

"Paper-knife, Your Majesty?" said the man in rags, in a mystified sort of way.

"Hmm. Never mind. Cheers."

"A thousand blessings be upon you."

"Quite. How are the vultures and everything?"

"Oh, the usual, you know."

"Not really."

"Oh, no, I suppose not. Well, let's see. It's Thursday, isn't it, so that means they just sort of sit there looking hungry. Friday being the traditional day for executions, as you know."

"Oh yes. Friday. Of course it is. Tell me . . . How do they, er . . . do it, exactly?"

"Well, that depends on your decrees, doesn't it?"

"Does it? Oh yes. Of course it does. Well, let's see, it's slipped my mind for the moment for some reason, what have I decreed for tomorrow, actually?"

"Tomorrow? Oh, not much, really. Couple of blasphemers, just the usual business with the hot irons, then there's one political for the crocodiles, don't know what he's done exactly, plus one embezzler of the imperial funds, which is mainly what I'm looking forward to."

"Why?"

"Oh, well, if its hands you see, then I get to keep the rings. If it's bracelets I usually toss for it with the executioner, but rings are definitely mine. And if its embezzlement, well, I haven't actually seen the gent, but you can usually count on something a bit sort of pricey if you know what I mean." And he grinned artfully.

"I don't often come across people like you," said the Sultan.

"But all I do is carry out your wise and just commands," said the man in rags.

"My dear fellow," said the Sultan wearily. "You really can't expect me to take an interest in all the little details. Really you can't. I mean, that's what people like you are there for, isn't it?" He considered the Keeper of the Vultures and Crocodiles. Actually, he didn't seem to be looking quite as ragged as usual. "You've got some new clothes," he said, to change the subject.

"What? Oh yes. Not bad, are they? Bit stained around the collar, but what can you expect, eh?"

"But . . . Well, I mean to say . . . is that where all your clothes come from?"

The man nodded cheerfully: "Clothes, shoes, the lot."

"But wait a minute. What about all the rings and bracelets and everything you were just telling me about? Surely you could just buy your clothes in the normal way, couldn't you? Not that I'm an expert, you know. I have a whole government department to take care of that aspect of things."

"Well, I do have my expenses."

"What do you . . . Oh yes. Yes, of course. Cheers."

Mwap-ey! Mwap-ey!
Oalla, oalla
Mwap-ey! Mwap-ey!
Oalla, oalla-ey.

Call and response charm-song in the Argobba (?) language, said to ward off evil spirits during a girl's first menstruation. Repeated by the women of the tribe during the vigil over her confinement. Ethiopia, 1860s.

>> Bradley, *Compendium of Ethnography*, Chicago, 1928

A metal plate found in the centre of the Romanian town Jasa, covering an opening leading underground. It most likely depicts the 24 hours of the day. The plate possibly served as a calendar and sundial.

WHERE THE SILVER CAME FROM*

In China, the following story is told.

At the beginning of the world, there was no such thing as silver on earth or in heaven. But one day, Yu decided that he wished to be married, and so he looked for a bride. He looked in Heaven and in Earth, and eventually his eye fell upon the Princess A Xiao, who lived in the clouds, and who was more beautiful than any woman who had ever lived. But A Xiao's father was an official at the court of the Celestial Emperor, and he would not consent for his daughter to marry a mortal man. Yu went to him and piled great treasures at his feet: jade and pearls and all the rarest and most beautiful things there were in the world. But A Xiao's father looked at them with contempt, and would take none of them.

"I know that you are a great hero," he said to Yu. "But I will never permit my daughter to marry you, unless you can bring me a treasure that no-one in earth or heaven has ever seen before." And Yu went away, and he wept and wept, and his tears became the Pearl River and the Yellow River, but still A Xiao's father would not relent. And in the end Yu stopped his weeping, and realized that he would have to think of something.

Now at that time there lived a famous hermit, who was really the Immortal Xiu, and so Yu went to ask him for his help. The hermit was very angry to have his solitude disturbed like that, and he struck the ground with his staff. It broke into a thousand sticks, and the thousand sticks all flew through the air to beat Yu. But Yu blew a great breath, and the thousand sticks were blown away to nothing. But the hermit waved his hand, and Yu's breath turned into a whirlwind, that came to lift Yu up to heaven. But Yu clapped the whirlwind between his hands, and the whirlwind was dispersed to nothing in the air.

"What is it you want?" said the hermit, when he saw that he could not beat Yu

---

*Adapted from *Folk Tales Of South-West China*, ed. Wendy Wang, (Hong Kong: Phoenix Publishing Corp., 1987).

by strength or by magic. "Can't you see that I do not wish to be disturbed?"

"I must have a treasure that no-one on earth or in heaven has ever seen before," said Yu. "And so I have come to beg for your advice."

"My advice?" said the hermit. "And what will you give me in return?"

"What would you like to have in return?" said Yu.

"I would only ask you to return my solitude to me," said the hermit.

"You shall have it," said Yu, prostrating himself.

"Very well. But I warn you, it will not be so easy for you to find this treasure."

"I am ready," said Yu.

"Very well. The first thing you must do is go and see the Dragon of the North Wind. He is gold and green and very wise. And you must bring back the Pearl of Wisdom to me. He holds it in his jaws. And now please leave me alone."

"Thank you," said Yu. And he travelled for many, many *li*, until he reached the palace of the Dragon of the North Wind. He pounded on the door until the earth shook; but nobody came. He pounded on the door until the sky shook; but still nobody came. He pounded on the door until the earth and the sky shook together; and at last a servant came and opened the door a crack.

"Go away," he said. "My master is sleeping."

"If you do not let me in I will tear your palace down!" said Yu. "For I must see your master." And he pushed the servant aside and strode into the hall where the Dragon of the North Wind sat on his throne.

"My name is Yu," he said. "And I must have the Pearl of Wisdom from you."

"What will you give me in return?" said the Dragon of the North Wind.

"In return I will give you a treasure that no-one in heaven or earth has ever seen before," said Yu. The Dragon of the North Wind considered him.

"Where is this treasure, and what is it called?" he asked eventually.

"It has no name yet, and as to where it is, that is something I cannot tell you."

"I see that you do not have it yet," said the Dragon of the North Wind. "But I will let you take the Pearl of Wisdom anyway, for I would like to have a treasure that no-one in earth or heaven has ever seen before. So take the Pearl from my

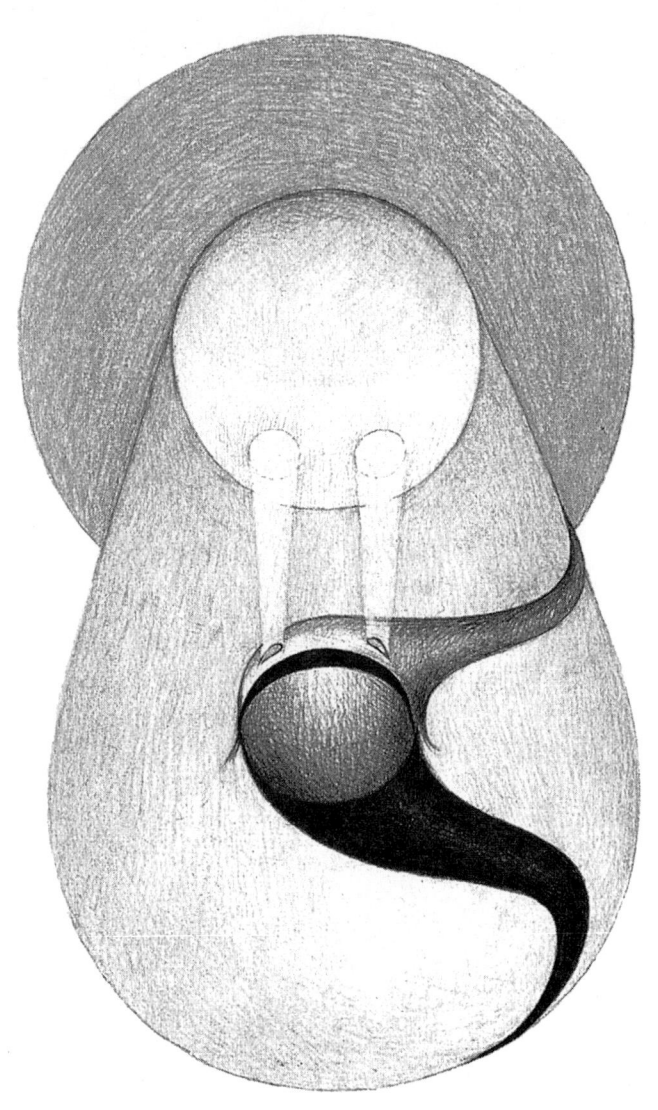

jaws, and I hope it will help you."

"Thank you," said Yu. And he took the Pearl of Wisdom back to the hermit and told him what had happened.

"Next you must go to see the Dragon of the West Wind, said the hermit. He is gold and red, and very fierce. And you must bring back the Sword of Victory to me. He holds it in his jaws. And now please leave me alone."

"Thank you," said Yu. And he travelled for many *li* until he reached the palace of the Dragon of the West Wind. He pounded on the door until the sun stopped in the sky to listen; but nobody came. He pounded on the door until the moon stopped in the sky to listen; but still nobody came. He pounded on the door until the sun and the moon together stopped to listen; and at last a servant came and opened the door a crack.

"My master is sleeping!" he said, in an angry voice. "Please go away!"

"If you do not let me in I will tear your palace down," said Yu. "For I must see your master!" And he pushed the servant aside and strode into the hall where the Dragon of the West Wind sat on his throne.

"My name is Yu," he said. "And I must have the Sword of Victory from you."

"Then you will have to fight me for it!" said the Dragon of the West Wind. And Yu and the Dragon of the West Wind fought all day and all night. They broke a hundred swords and a hundred lances, and Yu gave the Dragon of the West Wind a hundred wounds, and the Dragon of the West Wind gave Yu a hundred wounds. But in the end the Dragon of the West Wind was exhausted.

"Enough!" he cried. "Here is the Sword of Victory for you." And Yu took the Sword of Victory from his jaws and carried it back to the hermit.

"Now you must go and see the Dragon of the South Wind. He is gold and yellow and very rich. And you must bring back to me the Jade of Wealth. He holds it in his jaws. And now please leave me."

"Thank you," said Yu. And he travelled for many *li* until he reached the palace of the Dragon of the South Wind. He went to knock on the door, but a servant in a coat of diamonds opened it at once.

"My master is expecting you," he said. "Come in." And Yu strode into the hall where the Dragon of the South Wind was sitting on his throne.

"My name is Yu," he said. "And I must have the Jade of Wealth from you."

"But the Jade of Wealth is a treasure beyond price," said the Dragon of the South Wind. "Why should I give it to you? What will be my profit?"

"I know nothing about profit," said Yu.

"Ah. Well, in that case, let us make a bargain. I understand that you are searching for a treasure that no-one in earth or heaven has ever seen before, and furthermore, that you have already agreed to share this treasure with the Dragon of the North Wind."

"That's right," said Yu.

"I know. Well, I will allow you to take the Jade of Wealth from me as long as you agree that when you have found your treasure, you will divide it up into four parts. You will take one part, the Dragon of the North Wind will take one part, and you will give the remaining two parts to me. Agreed?"

"I suppose so."

"Here you are then." And Yu took the Jade of Wealth back to the hermit and explained what had happened.

"Now you must go to see the Dragon of the East Wind. He is gold and blue and he knows everything. And you must bring back to me the Cauldron of Knowledge. And now please leave me."

"Thank you," said Yu. He travelled many, many *li*, and when he arrived at the palace, the Dragon of the East Wind was waiting for him.

"My name is Yu," he said.

"I know," said the Dragon of the East Wind. "And I know what you want from me. But the Cauldron of Knowledge contains all the knowledge in the world. So you must tell me where I can put it instead; and if you can do that, then I will let you borrow the Cauldron for a while." So Yu tore down the sky and made a bag of it, and then he emptied all the knowledge from the Cauldron into the bag and tied it up with a comet's tail. And then he said to the Dragon of the East Wind:

"Now I will take your Cauldron for a little while."

"Very well," said the Dragon of the East Wind. And Yu took the Cauldron of Knowledge back to the hermit.

"Good," said the hermit. "Now we are ready. Please make a fire." And so Yu reached up into heaven and took some fire from the sun to heat the Cauldron. And the hermit threw the Pearl of Wisdom and the Sword of Victory and the Jade of Wealth into the Cauldron. "You must heat the Cauldron for a day and a night," he said, "And then your treasure will be ready. But please do not speak to me, for my only wish is for you to leave me alone." So Yu heated the Cauldron, and after a day and a night he saw that the Pearl and the Sword and the Jade had all fused together into a treasure that no-one in heaven or on earth had ever seen before. He tipped it out of the Cauldron onto the ground and looked at it.

"What is it?" he said.

"It is called *silver*," said the hermit. And Yu took the silver and he divided it up into four parts. He gave one part to the Dragon of the North Wind, and he gave two parts to the Dragon of the South Wind, and he returned the Cauldron of Knowledge to the Dragon of the East Wind. He undid the bag he had made, and put all the knowledge back into the Cauldron, and then he put the sky back where it belonged. But he kept the comet's tail for A Xiao so she could wear it in her hair.

"We have made silver," he said.

"I know," said the Dragon of the East Wind. "It is made from the Pearl of Wisdom and the Sword of Victory and the Jade of Wealth. And now you will be able to go to heaven and give it to A Xiao's father. And now that there is silver in the world, men will use it to buy and sell everything that they can see. For that is its magic. They will be able to buy and sell everything in the world except for knowledge alone, for that did not go into its making."

And Yu took the silver to the palace in the clouds where A Xiao lived with her father. He kept some of it for himself, but made most of it into bracelets and necklaces for A Xiao to wear at her wedding. And little by little, as time went by, she used the silver to buy things for herself and for Yu; so that the silver was spread all over the world.

And that is where the silver came from.

THE SULTAN AND THE MAN IN RAGS FOR THE LAST TIME

The Keeper of the Sultan's Women and the Keeper of the Sultan's Treasure and the Keeper of the Sultan's Hawks and Hounds were now very worried. Their plan, after all, had been perfectly simple – but now it had gone wrong, and there was nothing they could do about it. They knew from past experience that the Sultan would sometimes get so bored or depressed or angry or whatever it was that the only cure for it was to have someone sent to the crocodiles. That always seemed to do the trick, for some reason; and they all knew that the Doctor had had a narrow escape. What they usually did was to provide a ready-made victim for the Sultan's bad temper, and the "Keeper of the Crocodiles" idea had looked like a good one. Just someone to blame was all they needed; and so they had sent for a common criminal and told him that if he didn't do what they said they'd have him flayed alive. But they had reckoned without the man's ability to tell outrageous lies, that was the problem... And now things were just going from bad to worse. The Sultan was sending for the man in rags more and more regularly, and they just had to go along with it. How could they tell him that he was just a common criminal from the dungeons? And now it seemed that the Sultan was getting more and more addicted to the man's stupid stories, and (scandalously!) to drinking nasty cheap brandy and resinated wine with him as well.

"We must do something!" said the Keeper of the Women.

"Absolutely!" said the Keeper of the Treasure.

"I agree!" said the Keeper of the Hawks and Hounds. And so they agreed on a new plan. Bribery! It had never failed them in the past, after all. And of course the Keeper of the Sultan's Vultures and Crocodiles was pleased to discover this change in their attitude towards him. "Dear sir," they started calling him. "Our esteemed friend." That sort of thing. He moved out of his damp and rat-infested cell into some comfortable apartments; and it wasn't long before he was going about in silk and brocade and jewels just like them. For now that he had the Sultan's ear, he found to his delight that there were suddenly all sorts of people who wanted to be his friend, starting with the miserable Doctor, who was easily convinced that his whole life and future now depended on whether the Keeper of the Crocodiles would be able to change the Sultan's mind about having him tortured to death or something. The Sultan and his new friend indulged themselves in ever longer and ever more frequent boozing sessions; and alas and alack for human nature – in the end they forgot completely about the stories. But the Sultan, who was not so stupid as he looked, could see perfectly well that the man's rags were getting less and less ragged as time went by. Before long, he noticed that the man had started wearing a nice gold signet ring with a tasteful little crocodile motif, and he realized that Keeper of the Vultures and Crocodiles must have become a position of some importance in the palace hierarchy. He even made a little joke about it.

"I've been thinking," he said one day, as he watched the Keeper of the Vultures and Crocodiles arranging his extravagant robes about him.

"Yes, sire?" said the man absent-mindedly.

"Well, now that you've been spending a bit more time around the palace, I thought perhaps it was about time we did something about your position."

"My position?" said the Keeper of the Crocodiles warily.

"Yes, yes. You remember. You wanted me to lift this terrible curse from the shoulders of your family, didn't you? I mean, I seem to remember you saying something like that." And the Sultan looked at his bejewelled friend with a look of bland enquiry.

"Ah," said the Keeper of the Sultan's Crocodiles. But of course the last thing he wanted now was to be stripped of his lucrative and advantageous position. He was even enjoying an occasional visit to the crocodile pond nowadays – when he had a political enemy to dispose of or something.

"Oh well," said the Sultan vaguely. "It was just a thought. I suppose we can leave it until some other time. Just say the word, though." And he smiled bleakly. "My dear fellow."

Well, in the end the Sultan became tired of drinking Armenian brandy with the Keeper of his Vultures and Crocodiles. And one day, he said in a tearful voice, "You know, today I feel terribly lonely."

"Oh, no!" said the Keeper of the Sultan's Women.

"Oh, no!" said the Keeper of the Sultan's Treasure.

"Oh, no!" said the Keeper of the Sultan's Hawks and Hounds.

"Oh, no!" said the Keeper of the Sultan's Vultures and Crocodiles.

And they all shook their heads very gravely.

Fierce fighting broke out between Rahwana's army and Rama Wijaya's army of monkeys, with both sides using magic weapons.

The Adventures of the Ape Envoy Hanoman Duta
Semarang, Central Java, 1996

THE CATFISH AND THE THUNDER

One day, the catfish was proceeding as usual, sniffing his way slowly and methodically along through the mud and slime of life, in search of some wonderful thing called Love, which he had never seen, and which he wasn't sure he would even recognize if he found it, when he heard a huge booming sound in the sky. BOOM! it went. And in a little while BOOM! it went again. "Well, I wonder what that can be?" thought the catfish to himself. "Oh! Perhaps it is the voice of Love! I had better find out if I can." And so he decided to ask all the creatures that he met to see if they knew anything about it.

The first creature he met was the eagle. The eagle was very proud.

"Excuse me," said the catfish. "Do you mind if I ask you a question?"

"You may ask me any question you like," said the eagle. "I fly so high in the sky that I can see the whole world spread out below me like a cloth spread out on a table. There is nothing that happens in the whole wide world that I do not know about."

"Well that is very convenient," said the catfish. "For I was wondering if you knew anything about the strange voice in the sky I heard a little while ago."

"A sort of booming sound, you mean?" said the eagle.

"That's it!" said the catfish. "That's it exactly."

"Well," said the eagle, a little doubtfully, "I have heard it, of course, many times, but . . . Well, what exactly was it that you wanted to know?"

"Oh, I was wondering if it might not be the voice of Love. For I have been searching for Love for a long time now."

"I suppose it is possible," said the eagle uncertainly. "But I'm afraid I usually concentrate more on rats and mice and that sort of thing."

"I see," said the catfish, in a disappointed sort of voice. "Well, thank you anyway." And he continued on his way.

"Hello," said the next creature that the catfish happened to meet. It was an upside-down flamingo, of course. "What can I do for you?" it said. But the catfish couldn't understand what it was saying.

"I don't understand what you are saying," he said; and the flamingo stood upright to talk to him.

"What can I do for you?" it said.

"What a strange creature you are!" said the catfish. "Well, since you ask, I am trying to find out about a strange booming sound that I heard in the sky a while ago. I thought that perhaps it might be the voice of Love."

"Love?" said the flamingo. "Is that what it sounds like? Well I never. Learn something new every day, don't you? My, my."

"No, no," said the catfish quickly. "I don't know if that's really what it is. I'm trying to find out, that's all."

"Oh, well, in that case I'm afraid there's no point in asking me. I am universally recognized to be a creature of very limited intelligence, and so I'm afraid I'd be quite useless for assistance in any such investigation as the one you describe. But I suppose I could make another suggestion."

"What's that?"

"Well, if you can wait until this evening, there is one particular bird you might ask. His name is Owl, and he is very wise and intelligent and clever. You will recognize him by his screeching. Too wit to woo is what he chiefly says."

"Thank you," said the catfish.

"Don't mention it," said the flamingo.

Well, that evening the catfish was able to ask the owl what he thought about it all.

"Too wit to woo!" said the owl. "What a strange question!"

"But what is the answer?" insisted the catfish.

"You must find a river of tears," said the owl. "And once every hundred years, there is a slave-girl who comes to wash blankets there. You must ask her about it, too wit to woo. That's all I know about it, anyway." And with that, the owl flapped off into the darkness.

Well, it took a long time of course, but eventually the catfish found his way into the river of tears, and by chance the very next day the slave-girl the owl had told him about came down to wash her blankets there, just as the owl had said.

"Hello," said the catfish.

"Hello," said the slave-girl suspiciously. She didn't like talking fish, for some reason. "What do you want?"

"I want to know about the voice in the sky that sometimes calls out with a great booming sound."

"The thunder, you mean?" said the slave-girl, a little crossly.

"What's that?" said the catfish.

"Yes, yes, it must be the thunder you're talking about. No question of that."

"Oh. Well, can you tell me where it comes from?" went on the catfish, eagerly.

"From Thunder Mountain, of course. Everybody knows that!"

"And can you tell me how to get there?"

"Just follow this river until you come to a big black mountain with no trees on it. That's the place."

"Oh, thank you so much!" said the catfish. "Now I'll be able to find Love! I'm sure of it!" And he continued on his way.

Well, in a little while he came to the big black mountain with no trees on it that the slave-girl had described. But there was no-one in sight, and he couldn't hear the thunder either, and so he just swam round and round, wondering what to do next. But suddenly *Flip*! someone had caught him in a net, and *Flop*! there he was swimming around in the bottom of a bucket.

"There!" said a voice. "Now, I think you'll be very nice grilled with some lemon. I wonder if we have any."

"Oh, no," said the catfish quickly. "I think there must be some sort of mistake. Don't you know that I am a horrible Poisonfish from Persia, and that just one little taste of me would certainly kill you?"

"Really?" said the voice. "Well I never. Let's take a look at you then." And a strange old woman leaned over the bucket and looked in at him. "Well, well. I've never seen a Persian Poisonfish before. But I must say, they do say that the Poisonfish is especially dangerous."

"Oh yes," said the catfish. "Deadly."

"Hmm. Well, in that case, I suppose I won't grill you after all."

"Oh good."

"Instead, I'll take you to my master the King of Thunder Mountain, and he can use you to guard his treasure. He has a great collection of spiders and snakes and scorpions and things like that. But I don't think he has a Persian Poisonfish. I'm sure he'll be pleased."

"But . . . "

"Yes?"

"Oh, nothing. Let's go." And the old woman picked up the bucket and carried the catfish all the way up the mountain to the very top, where there was a magic castle with walls of silver and gold. A tall man came out to meet them.

"What have you got there?" he said.

"A Persian Poisonfish!" said the woman, sounding pleased.

"Oh, good. Just what we need," said the man, but he didn't sound very enthusiastic, actually. He took the bucket and examined the catfish. "Hmm. Very well, that will be all. Thank you." The woman went off, grumbling a little to herself, for she had been expecting some kind of reward.

"Well, my friend," said the King of Thunder Mountain. "You had better explain yourself, and be quick about it! For you are no more a Persian Poisonfish than I am. So you had better tell me exactly what your business is here, or else I shall be forced to have you thrown in with the snakes and spiders and scorpions anyway. So let's hear it."

"Kind sir," said the catfish. "I admit it was all nothing but a subterfuge and a pretence. But please don't throw me in with the noxious beasts you mention. For I am simply searching for Love and nothing else."

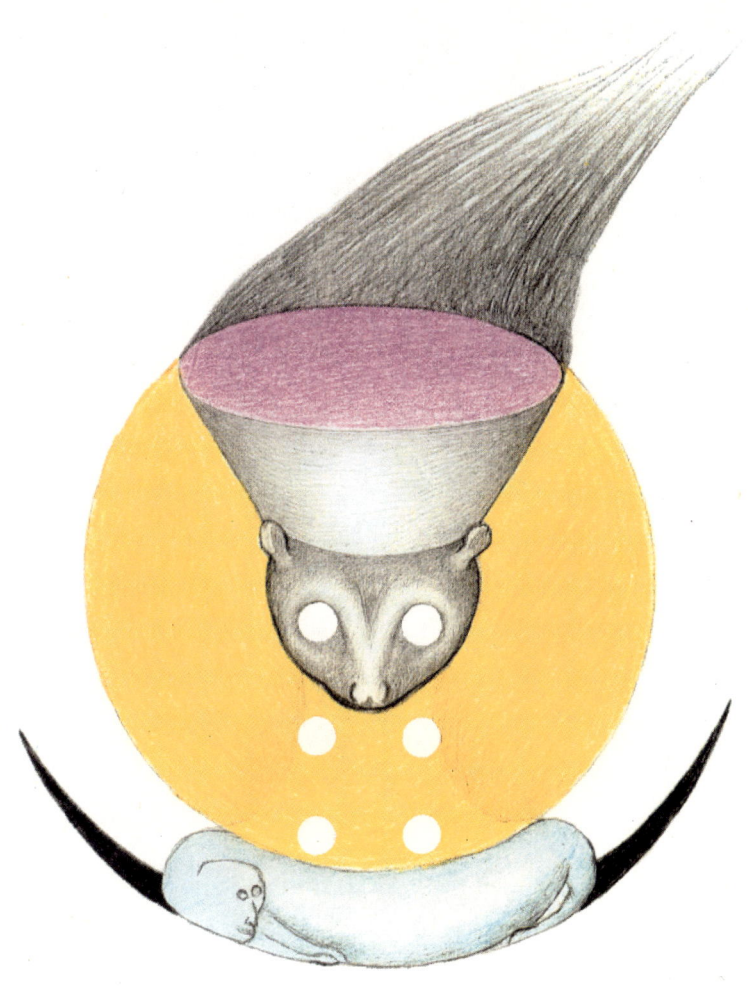

"Love?" said the king incredulously. "Then what on earth are you doing here?"

"Well," said the catfish, trying not to sound too foolish. "I heard this sound in the sky, you see. A sort of booming sound . . . "

"The thunder."

"If you say so. Only I didn't know anything about that. I had never heard it before, and I asked all the other creatures that I met, and none of them could tell me what it was, and so I tried to find it, because . . . "

"Yes?"

"Well, because I thought it might be the voice of Love. And I have been searching for Love for ever such a long time now." But the king let out a great roar of laughter.

"Love!" he repeated, laughing. "Oh, that is very good! *Love*, he says!" The catfish swam around miserably in his bucket.

"Yes," he said. "That's right. But I suppose I've just been wasting my time as usual."

"I suppose you could say that," said the king. But he spoke kindly now, and the catfish didn't feel so afraid. "Would you like to know where the thunder comes from?" he said. The catfish nodded. "Very well. I'll show you." And the king picked up the bucket and carried it along a narrow winding path, until they came to a secret cave with a magic door. The king said a magic word, and the door sprang open, and they went inside. The king carefully tipped the catfish out of the bucket into a crystal basin, and the catfish swam round and round in wonder. The whole of the inside of the cave seemed to be made of solid silver. There were silver chairs and tables, silver books and pictures, and the king put on a great silver crown and sat down grandly on a silver throne.

"It's all made of silver," said the catfish.

"That's right," said the king. "The whole mountain is made of silver. It's only black on the outside so that no-one knows. I am the richest king in the whole wide world! The King of Silver Mountain is my real name."

"And what about the thunder?" said the catfish.

"I was coming to that. Watch." And the king picked up a little silver bell and rang it. Two silver giants came in, carrying a huge silver horn. The king winked at the catfish, took a deep breath, and put the horn to his lips; and suddenly the whole mountain seemed to boom and shake.

"That's what I heard before!" said the catfish.

"I know," said the king, when the echoes had died away. At a gesture of his hand, the two silver giants took the thunder-horn away again. "It's for protection. A very long time ago, a gold and yellow dragon told me that if I wanted he would make me the richest king in the world. He said that if I wanted, he would give me so much silver that even if you took all the rest of the silver in the whole wide world and put it all together, it would still not even make one half of the silver that I would have at my disposal."

"Golly," said the catfish.

"Well, naturally I agreed at once, and so here I am. I am so rich that I can have silver books and silver paintings, silver tables and silver chairs, and in fact all the silver I want."

"Congratulations," said the catfish, looking round. "You certainly do seem to have a lot of silver."

"Yes." But the king frowned a little. "Now, I will admit that I should probably have studied the small print of our agreement a little more carefully."

"Ah."

"Yes. There was a clause on page seventeen I should really have paid more attention to."

"What did it say?"

"Oh. Well, it said that I agreed not to act in such a manner as to disrupt world silver prices. That's all. Sounded quite sensible, I thought."

"Yes."

"Except . . . Well, except it seems that now I can't actually do anything with it. All this silver, I mean. Except look after it, that is. And that's why I keep all the spiders and snakes and scorpions, you see. To frighten people away."

"And is that what the thunder's for, too?"

"Exactly. Makes everyone think the place is full of evil spirits."

"Ah." The catfish thought about this for a while. "So what are you going to do?"

"Do?" said the king unhappily. "Well, I suppose I shall just have to wait until the dragon decides that I can use some of the silver. He has someone working on it, he says."

"Oh good."

"Yes. Anyway, listen, there is something you could do for me, actually."

"Really?"

"Yes. You see, the thing is, I do get a bit, well, a bit lonely, sitting here year after year with only the old woman for company. Between you and me, I often think that she must be in the pay of the dragon. Spying on me, you know, to make sure I don't try and spend any of the silver. But what I mean to say is that I'd really be terribly grateful for some kind of break in the monotony of it all. And we could just eat you, you know. Grill you with lemon or something."

"What did you have in mind exactly?" said the catfish quickly.

"Well, I've always been rather fond of stories, actually," said the king. "You don't happen to know any, do you?"

"Oh, I think I might be able to manage that," said the catfish.

"Oh good!" said the king. "Only . . . Well, I don't really know what kind of story would be best."

"Oh, that's easy," said the catfish. "For there is only one story I know."

"And does it have a name, your story?" said the king.

"Oh yes," said the catfish. "The name of the story is *Amuwapi at the Beginning of the World.*"

AMUWAPI AT THE BEGINNING OF THE WORLD

At the beginning of the world there was only Amuwapi, and he was all alone. He wept and wept and wept, for he was really very lonely.

A frog saw him weeping and said, "Amuwapi, you should not weep like that. Look at me! I swim in the river all day, and I am happy." But Amuwapi said, "It would not put an end to my loneliness to be like you." And he sent the frog away.

A deer saw him weeping and said, "Amuwapi, you should not weep like that. Look at me! I run in the forest all day, and I am happy." But Amuwapi said, "It would not put an end to my loneliness to be like you." And he sent the deer away.

An ant saw him weeping and said, "Amuwapi, you should not weep like that. Look at me! I walk an invisible pathway, and I am happy." But Amuwapi said, "It would not put an end to my loneliness to be like you." And he sent the ant away.

Many, many years passed, and still Amuwapi did not stop weeping. And eventually, the sun stopped in the sky and came to speak to Amuwapi.

"Amuwapi!" said the sun. "I have watched you weeping since the beginning of the world, and you really should be ashamed of yourself. It is all your own fault, after all, if you feel lonely. So why don't you hide your face away in the Palace of the Moon, so that all the happy creatures in the world don't have to worry about you?"

"You are right," said Amuwapi. "That is what I will do." And so Amuwapi went away to live all alone in the Palace of the Moon, with only a single slave-girl to look after him, and that is where he will have to stay until the end of the world.

When the catfish had finished, the king looked at him for a long time. He seemed a bit disappointed with the story.

"Tell me," he said eventually. "Why is there no silver in your story?"

"I don't know," said the catfish. "Are there some stories with silver in them?"

"Oh, perhaps there are some such stories," said the king miserably. "Or perhaps it is only my story that has silver in it. I don't know. But thanks all the same for telling me your story. I suppose it is better than nothing. I will be able to consider it at my leisure, anyway. Which is considerable. But I'm afraid I must disappoint you. I cannot help you with your search. You will just have to keep trying on your own. I will call the woman and tell her to carry you back down to the river and set you free. But I'll have to cast a special magic spell over you so that you forget all about me and my magic mountain."

"Oh well," said the catfish fatalistically. "Never mind."

"But tell me . . . Is there anything I can offer you as a reward before you go?" They both looked around. "Apart from silver, of course."

But the catfish really couldn't think of anything at all.

Roman votive shield, one of three which, according to some scholars, hung on the altar in the Temple of Amuwapi. On the reverse side there is engraved the words: DOLOR ET LACRIMÆ. *The world was created from the pain and the tears of Amuwapi.*

Rama Wijaya wanders in voluntary exile, escorted only by his beautiful wife Shinta and his faithful brother Leksmana. While they are comforting each other in their misery, a golden deer appears from the forest. Shinta is spellbound by this golden deer and begs Rama Wijaya to catch it.

The Adventures of the Ape Envoy Hanoman Duta
Semarang, Central Java, 1996

A NOTE ON THE SOURCES

The religious practices of ancient peoples show striking similarities: so striking, indeed, that it is often tempting to interpret them as having some common origin in a previous system of beliefs. A case in point is the cult of Amuwapi, the proto-Semitic "weeping god". Amuwapi is related (at least in the imagination of some prehistorians) to Amu Wabi (阿姆瓦比), the Chinese "man in the moon", to the Egyptian Thoth (also associated with writing) and to the pre-Vedic Ámbu-pa, or "Lord of the Waters" of India. His symbolism, itself by all appearances a synthesis of who knows how many earlier mythologies, includes several familiar motifs: lunar and solar symbols, a slave-girl (or sometimes a daughter) who performs magical deeds and who pines for love, a lunar residence, constant weeping, and so on. In Mesopotamia, and allegedly also in the Indus Valley, the cult was associated with the sundial and with writing, but it is impossible to tell how or why this association should have arisen (at least until someone unearths some pre-Sumerian writing!).

The etymological and folkloric researches of Dunleavy and Klipsten in this field have produced a wealth of material, which they claim supports their thesis that some components of "the Amuwapi cycle" (as they term their material) have survived into modern and even into some contemporary societies. Since they would also extend the same mythological cycle back to Palaeolithic cave painting, it is not surprising that these claims have been treated with some scepticism in learned circles. Indeed, there are those who simply deny any reality at all for the "Amuwapi cycle", and who say that Dunleavy and Klipsten's collection relies on nothing more than a biased and contrived manipulation of unrelated materials, which are presented together solely in order to support Dunleavy and Klipsten's far-fetched hypothesis. Their epic (and now famous) journey around the world to collect these materials has even been held up to ridicule in a notorious but anonymous parody article, in which the great Dunleavy is caricatured as Don Quixote, and Klipsten as his faithful Sancho Panza. But this is not the place to take up the cudgels on their behalf.

Archaeology can provide us with something more solid, and here we find at least one thread of the Amuwapi story that we can unravel a little more confidently. This is the connection with human sacrifice. It is a thread which, thankfully, history has long ago broken (for there are no reliable eye-witness accounts of any such practices having survived into recent times), but we can certainly find material evidence of such rituals having formed part of the culture of Man from the very earliest times. Dunleavy and Klipsten's researches seem to reveal that common elements in the rituals of human sacrifice are to be found in artefacts from as far afield as South America, Australasia and Central Africa, and although many would question their whole approach to the subject, the archaeological evidence does seem to offer some support for their theory. We know that the Vedic texts of India stem from what was originally a cult of human sacrifice (transformed into a cult of fire-worship by the Brahmans), and Mesopotamia, the Indus Valley, and Shang Dynasty China all offer evidence of broadly similar practices; and in Europe the Celts at least are supposed to have continued with such practices until they were eventually suppressed by the power of Rome and the Christian church. The recent decipherment of the Mohenjo-Daro glyphic texts (especially the controversial "Ritual of Sacrifice", as it is known) throws additional light on the subject, since it now appears that the cult of Amuwapi, with a curious admixture of solar astronomy and human sacrifice, was the basis of religious life in the settled and successful civilization that flourished in the Indus Valley. The characteristic feature of the sacrifice involved (apart, that is, from the sheer number of the victims) is the removal of head, heart and hands during the ritual. Now, there is some evidence of similar mutilations from isolated sites all over the inhabited world (except Australia) from the Upper Palaeolithic period (c. 30-35,000 BC), and this has led some commentators (O'Toole, especially) to discuss the possibility of the transmission of a Neanderthal social ritual. This hypothesis, though, is too extreme even to be assessed by scholarship; and we do no more than note it here.

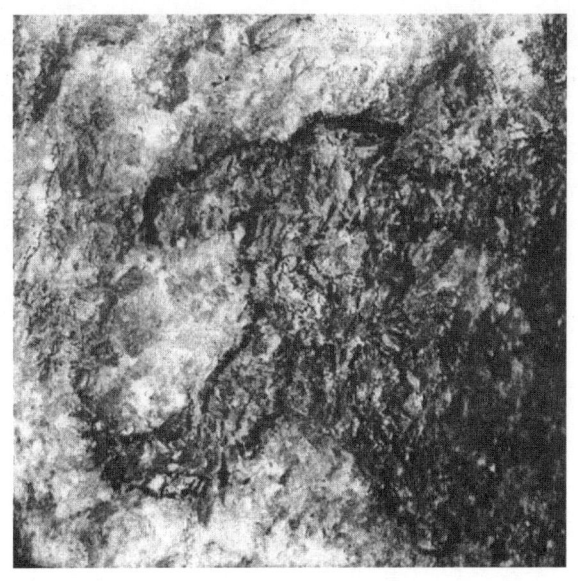

CAVE PAINTING: MAN WITH HEAD, HEART AND HANDS REMOVED.

Salamanca, Spain. c. 30 000 B.C.

A NOTE ON ETYMOLOGY

It has been generally accepted for a generation now that the derivation of the Canaanite (North Semitic) name *Amuwapi* and its variants can be traced back to a lost Sumerian original, reconstructed by Klipsten as Old Akkadian ᵈ*Amû(ḫ)a-pi-i*. It is pointed out that such a reconstruction would accord with the historical evidence for a cult of Amuwapi among the Sumerians, and would also connect with the Mohenjo-Daro glyphs and therefore with the pre-Vedic Indian *Ámbupa*, "Lord of the Waters", a title given to the god-king Varua; and all this is supposed to provide conclusive evidence in support of O'Toole's reconstruction of a cult of human sacrifice, transmitted from Mesopotamia to the Indus Valley, and thence to India and, via Central Asia, also to prehistoric China. But this reconstruction of events can certainly be questioned. In the first place, while the evidence for a Sumerian original is indeed convincing, on archaeological and historical grounds, Prof. Klipsten's reconstruction of the "original" Sumerian form is no more than a phonetically plausible transposition of much later Canaanite, Ugaritic and other materials back into Akkadian, and even this transposition relies on the fact that the elements *amû* and *a-pi-i* do occur — separately! — in Sumerian proper names of uncertain meaning found in unrelated Old Akkadian documents. Looking closely at Klipsten's evidence, we find that the Ugaritic and Hurrian sources he cites can in reality offer no more certain reading than *m-w-p*; whereas the account of a human sacrifice in the famous Uruk tablet Uk378e equally famously includes no proper name at all for the supposed target of the ritual. Greek and Sanskrit texts, while providing valuable mythological support, come from a much later stage of the name's etymology (if these connections are valid at all!). Looking at all these questions afresh, we are led to a different kind of account entirely. We may, I think, disregard Dunleavy's supposition that there is a direct connection between the Amuwapi of the Near East and the Amu Wabi of Central Asian and South Chinese folk tales — although there may be some conflation of mythological material, of course. As far as the "King Mu" of Zhou Dynasty China is concerned, Dunleavy simply disregards the fact that the "Book of Dreams," which is the only source for the supposed connection here, is itself widely supposed to be nothing but a Ming Dynasty forgery! No: let us return to the etymology of the name itself. While the Akkadian tablets so far deciphered have not provided direct evidence for a Sumerian or indeed for any other Mesopotamian original, internal evidence of cultural transmission does lead us in that direction. However, the cuneiform (𒊩), which is read in Akkadian as *amû*, the Sumerian proper name element noted by Klipsten, may also (*vide* Delitzsch, *Sumerisches Glossar*, Leipzig, 1914, pg. 11) be read as the Sumerian *ama* (Akkadian *ammu*), meaning "mother" — as in the Akkadian loan-word compound Ak. *ama'irrû* (Sum. *ama'irrukku*) — "wailing woman", or in various Akkadian loan-word compounds of Sum. *amā.lu(l)* — "goddess". In other words, we must take the small but significant step of realizing that "Amuwapi" has somehow changed sex in the process of her/his cultural transmission! We may therefore amend Klipsten's formulation of the reconstructed Sumerian original to Sum. ᵈ*Ama.api*, possibly (*pace* Klipsten!) via Old Akkadian ᵈ*Ammu(ḫ)a-pi-i*. While we can still make nothing of Klipsten's *a-pi-i*, either in Sumerian or in Semitic vocabularies, we could, for completeness, suppose a connection with Proto-Indo-European *u̯ābiō* — "shout, call, cry" (Hittite *wapiya* — "bark"; Umbrian *vapi* — "prophet"; Slovene *vápiti* — "to lament"; Old Czech *vabit* — "to summon"; Ukranian *vabyty* — "to enchant, to conjure"; Old Norse *œpa* — "to cry, to weep"; Old English *wēpan* — "to weep" etc., etc.), to give us a much more satisfactory etymology, i.e., *Amuwapi* — "Mother of Lamentation". We can surely find further anthropological (or gynaecological!) support for this construction in the association of the Amuwapi cult with the ritual seclusion of women, and indeed with Amuwapi's solitary residence in the Palace of the Moon, which looks to be more or less the same thing at root. Finally, let us remember that many of the Sumerian loan-words in Akkadian texts come from the *eme.sal* or "women's speech", and that Sumerian *dingir* (i.e. the determinant noted here as ᵈ⁾ means "god" or "goddess" interchangeably (nouns in Sumerian having no gender): and the story looks reasonably complete. Klipsten and Dunleavy's weeping god is revealed as the mere shadow of his tremendous Stone Age predecessor, the Mother of Lamentation, who took a tribute of (male?) hands, hearts and heads for uncounted ages past; and the cult itself as we know it, i.e. in its masculinized form, could plausibly now be interpreted as the means by which its own matriarchal predecessor was eventually overpowered and tamed. And how, we ask, can scholarship have missed the mark by so wide a margin? Let us recall the wise words of Sir Monier Monier-Williams, Fellow of Balliol College and Boden Professor of Sanskrit in the University of Oxford, who, in the Introduction to his great Sanskrit-English dictionary of 1899, laments himself, as follows.

> "Sincerity obliges me to confess that, during my long literary career, my mind has had to pass through a kind of painful discipline involving a gradual weakening of faith in the trustworthiness of my fellow men . . . till now, that I have arrived at the end of my journey, I find myself left with my faith in the accuracy of human beings generally — and certainly not excepting myself — somewhat distressingly disturbed."

Eventually the catfish decided that there was no such thing as Love to be found anywhere in the whole wide world. He had searched for it in every sea and lake and river and ditch that there was, and he had never once even seen it. But since he had nothing else to do, he still kept on looking.

And one day, he was making his way along the bottom of a very muddy deep dark pond (which reminded him, actually, of the one he had lived in all alone for so many years) when suddenly, he bumped his head against something soft. It was a big grey soft sort of thing, he could see, and it seemed strangely familiar for some reason. The water was very murky, though, and he really couldn't make out what sort of thing it was, but still, there was something about it that made his heart beat faster, and his tail flicked itself from side to side with a sort of nervous excitement.

"Can't you look where you're going?" said a voice, and though it was a cross and bad-tempered sort of voice in a way, still there was something strangely soft and inviting in it.

"Who are you?" he said, and he found he had a lump in his throat when he said it.

"I'm a catfish, of course!" said the voice. "Don't you know anything?"

> And the catfish suddenly realized what it was
> that he had been searching for.

THE BOOK OF AMUWAPI
CHRISTOPHER LORD

Color illustrations by Petr Nikl
Slave-girl pendant on cover by Anna-Riitta Lord and Nicola Ascoli
Design by Chaim
Limited first edition of 1,000 copies published in 2000 by
Twisted Spoon Press / P.O. Box 21 – Preslova 12 / 150 21 Prague 5 /
Czech Republic / twispoon@terminal.cz
Printed and bound in the Czech Republic by Tiskárny Havlíčkův Brod
We thank Ken Ganfield, Michaela Hájková, Vladislav Zadrobílek
and Studio Forma for their generous assistance.
Distributed by Subterranean Co.: P.O. Box 160, South Fifth Street,
Monroe, OR 97456 USA (subco@clipper.net) / Small Press Distribution:
1341 Seventh Street, Berkeley, CA 94710-1409 USA (orders@spdbooks.org) /
Marginal Distribution: 277 George St. N., Unit 103, Peterborough, Ontario
K9J 3G9 CAN (marginal@ptbo.igs.net)